VOLUME 3

Getting dinner on the table quickly means more time to enjoy a meal with family and friends! Just like its predecessors, the 3rd volume of *29 Minutes to Dinner* provides fix-it-fast dinners for any night of the week. Chapters include poultry, fish & seafood, beef & pork and meatless, so there's something for everyone.

Flip the pages to quickly see how long each recipe will take from start to finish–many can be done in even *less* than 29 minutes! Our *Smart Ideas for Quick Cooking (p. 4-5)* show you just how easy it is to make satisfying meals at home, and will inspire you to do it more often!

So, what's for dinner? It's only 29 minutes away!

Enjoy!

The Pampered Chef® Test Kitchens

Contents

Oven-Fried Chicken with Grilled Waffle Sticks p. 9

poultry

A true dinnertime staple, the convenience of poultry means endless mealtime possibilities. Bring new life to chicken and turkey with our quick-fix meal ideas that feed a family fast.

6

Sautéed Halibut with Arugula Salad p. 43

fish & seafood

Be fearless with fish! Anything but intimidating; these simple seafood dishes will show you just how easy it is to make fish and seafood that everyone at the table will love.

40

22 minutes

Japanese Steakhouse Pork Chops p. 67

beef & pork

Short on time? It won't stop you from enjoying satisfying beef and pork dishes. With time-saving cuts of meat, you can even make a hearty stew in minutes.

64

25 minutes

Linguine with Creamy Asparagus Pesto p. 105

meatless

Spice up your dinnertime regime with a variety of vegetarian plates, including family favorites and out of the ordinary entrées. All without a morsel of meat!

102

Smart Ideas for Quick Cooking

Let these practical techniques show you how to make the most of your time in the kitchen.

1
What takes the longest? Start that first.

2
Get the most from your microwave!

3
Scoop up some extra time!

4
Punch up the flavor!

Start foods that take longer to cook like rice and pasta *first*, so they'll be hot and ready by the time the recipe is finished. Begin cooking the spaghetti before preparing the sauce, like in *Spaghetti with Fresh Tomato Clam Sauce (p. 47)*.

Get a head start by precooking potatoes in the microwave. Use the extra time to prepare other ingredients in your recipe, like in *Lemon Pepper Chicken & Crispy Potatoes (p. 35)*.

Scoops are a great way to evenly divide burger, meatball or patty mixtures. Not only do they save time, but scoops ensure that portions are even in size and shape, allowing them to cook evenly like in *Couscous Cakes with Cucumber Salad (p. 125)*.

Cook with full-flavored ingredients like fresh garlic, onion, fresh lemon zest and juice to add major kick to recipes, like in *Cavatappi & Meatballs in Lemon-Basil Sauce (p. 25)*.

5

Pound meat thin–it cooks faster.

Pounding meat thinner prior to cooking not only makes it cook faster, but it tenderizes it as well. Try *Steak Fajita Burritos (p. 75)* and see for yourself.

6

Two boards are better than one!

Recipes that call for meat and vegetables are easier to prepare by keeping two cutting boards on hand. Use one for meat and the other for vegetables. This prevents cross-contamination and saves time by not having to wash your cutting board in between steps. See *Middle Eastern-Style Beef Pops (p. 87)*.

7

Pizza faster than delivery? Start the crust first!

Get your pizza crust baking in the oven while you prepare pizza toppings. This way, you'll get a crispy crust and have ample time to prepare the toppings, like in *Spicy Thin-Crust Sausage Pizza (p. 77)*.

8

Wipe out the skillet and press onward!

When recipes call to make different components in the same skillet, there's no need to wash the skillet several times. Just grab two folded paper towels with tongs, wipe the skillet clean and continue the recipe. A hot pan will reduce additional time needed to preheat. See how easy it is in *Saucy Chorizo & Egg Tostadas (p. 93)*.

Smoky Cheddar-Stuffed Turkey Sliders p. 33

Asian BBQ Chicken Drumsticks p. 17

Hazelnut-Crusted Turkey with Cannellini Salad p. 21

Cavatappi & Meatballs in Lemon-Basil Sauce p. 25

poultry
DISHES

Cook up a variety of weeknight dinners featuring versatile chicken and turkey.

Oven-Fried Chicken with Grilled Waffle Sticks

Yield: 6 servings

This fun version of a southern favorite features an easy waffle made right in the Grill Pan.

1. Preheat oven to 425°F (220°C). For chicken, mix first six ingredients in first **Coating Tray** until thoroughly blended.

2. Pour buttermilk into second tray. Dip chicken into buttermilk and then into spice mixture, coating evenly.

3. Arrange chicken evenly on **Medium Sheet Pan**. Spray chicken with canola oil using **Kitchen Spritzer**. Bake chicken 20-23 minutes or until internal temperature reaches 165°F (74°C) in thickest part of chicken.

4. Meanwhile, for waffle sticks, heat **Grill Pan** over medium heat 3 minutes. Combine all ingredients except syrup in **Stainless (2-qt./2-L) Mixing Bowl**; whisk until smooth.

5. Pour batter into pan; cook 4-6 minutes or until bottom is golden brown and bubbles appear on the top. Using **Nylon Panini Spatula**, loosen edges and bottom of waffle and carefully turn over. Cook an additional 2-3 minutes or until golden brown.

6. Remove chicken from oven. Cut waffle into eight rectangles. Slice each rectangle into thirds.

7. Serve chicken with waffle sticks. Drizzle with maple syrup.

Chicken

⅓   cup (75 mL) flour
1½ tbsp (22 mL) paprika
1½ tbsp (22 mL) garlic powder
1   tbsp (15 mL) onion powder
1   tsp (5 mL) salt
½   tsp (2 mL) cayenne pepper
1   cup (250 mL) buttermilk
6   bone-in, skin-on chicken thighs (6 oz/175 g each)

Waffle Sticks

¾   cup (175 mL) flour
¼   cup (50 mL) cornstarch
½   tsp (2 mL) salt
½   tsp (2 mL) baking powder
¼   tsp (1 mL) baking soda
1   cup (250 mL) buttermilk
1   egg
⅓   cup (75 mL) canola oil
¾   cup (175 mL) pure maple syrup

Cook's Tips:

If desired, regular pancake syrup can be substituted for the pure maple syrup.

It's no mistake – you don't need to add any oil to the Grill Pan when preparing the waffle sticks. The oil in the batter combined with a hot Grill Pan will prevent sticking.

U.S. Nutrients per serving (1 chicken thigh and 4 waffle sticks): **Calories** 640, **Total Fat** 34 g, **Saturated Fat** 7 g, **Cholesterol** 145 mg, **Sodium** 870 mg, **Carbohydrate** 57 g, **Fiber** 2 g, **Protein** 25 g

U.S. Diabetic exchanges per serving: 3 Starch, 1 Fruit, 2 High-Fat Meat, 3 Fat (4 Carb)

Chicken 'N Gnocchi Soup

Frozen gnocchi is a quick alternative for the traditional dumplings usually found in this hearty soup.

Yield: 6 servings
(about 8 cups/2 L)

1	small rotisserie chicken (about 3 cups/750 mL shredded)
⅓	cup (75 mL) canola oil, divided
1	pkg (16 oz/450 g) frozen potato gnocchi (do not thaw, see Cook's Tip)
4	garlic cloves, pressed and divided
1	tbsp (15 mL) butter
½	medium onion
1	celery rib
1	medium carrot
½	medium zucchini
8	fresh sage leaves
6	cups (1.5 L) chicken stock
	Grated fresh Parmesan cheese (optional)

1. Remove chicken from bones and shred; set aside.

2. Heat *¼ cup (50 mL)* of the oil in **11-** or **12-in. (28-** or **30-cm) Skillet** over medium heat 1-3 minutes or until shimmering. Add gnocchi and *2* of the garlic cloves pressed with **Garlic Press**; cook 5-6 minutes, stirring frequently until golden brown.

3. Add butter to Skillet; stir gently until butter melts. Remove Skillet from heat and set aside.

4. Chop onion, celery and carrot using **Food Chopper**. Heat remaining 1 tbsp (15 mL) oil in **(4-qt./3.8-L) Casserole** over medium-high heat 1-3 minutes or until shimmering. Add onion, celery, carrot and remaining 2 garlic cloves; cook 3-4 minutes, stirring frequently.

5. Chop zucchini and sage using Food Chopper. Add zucchini, sage, stock and chicken to Casserole. Cover and bring to a simmer; cook 4-5 minutes or until heated through.

6. Ladle soup into serving bowls; top with gnocchi. Sprinkle Parmesan over soup, if desired.

Cook's Tips:

The gnocchi should be added to the Skillet *frozen* in this recipe. Frozen gnocchi browns nicely and prevents the insides from overcooking and turning gummy.

If desired, 2 tsp (10 mL) dried sage can be substituted for the fresh sage.

U.S. Nutrients per serving (about 1⅓ cups/325 mL): **Calories** 420, **Total Fat** 19 g, **Saturated Fat** 4 g, **Cholesterol** 55 mg, **Sodium** 840 mg, **Carbohydrate** 36 g, **Fiber** 3 g, **Protein** 25 g

U.S. Diabetic exchanges per serving: 2½ Starch, 2½ Lean Meat, 2 Fat (2½ Carb)

Crunchy Chicken Chile Relleno Tacos

27 minutes

The combined flavors of authentic Mexican stuffed peppers make taco night extra special!

Yield: 6 servings

1½ lbs (700 g) boneless, skinless chicken breasts
2 tbsp (30 mL) canola oil, divided
2 tbsp (30 mL) **Tex-Mex Rub**
12 hard taco shells
1 poblano pepper
1 medium onion
2 garlic cloves, pressed
2 cups (500 mL) shredded Chihuahua cheese
1 cup (250 mL) green enchilada sauce
½ cup (125 mL) fresh cilantro

1. Preheat oven to 375°F (190°C). Slice chicken into ½-in. (1-cm) strips using **Chef's Knife**.

2. Heat *1 tbsp (15 mL)* of the oil in **11-** or **12-in. (28-** or **30-cm) Skillet** over medium-high heat 1-3 minutes or until shimmering. Meanwhile, combine chicken, rub and remaining 1 tbsp (15 mL) oil in **Classic Batter Bowl**; mix well.

3. Add chicken to Skillet. Cook undisturbed 3-4 minutes or until browned. Arrange taco shells in **Small Ridged Baker**. Bake 3-4 minutes or until crisp.

4. Thinly slice poblano and onion. Add poblano, onion and garlic pressed with **Garlic Press** to Skillet. Cook an additional 4-5 minutes or until vegetables are softened, stirring occasionally.

5. Remove baker from oven. Sprinkle half of the cheese into bottoms of taco shells. Stir sauce into Skillet. Bring to a simmer and remove from heat.

6. Fill taco shells with chicken mixture using **Chef's Tongs**. Top with remaining cheese.

7. Bake tacos an additional 1-2 minutes or until cheese is melted. Chop cilantro and sprinkle over tacos.

Cook's Tip:

If desired, taco seasoning mix can be substituted for the Tex-Mex Rub and Monterey Jack cheese can be substituted for the Chihuahua cheese.

U.S. Nutrients per serving (2 tacos): **Calories** 450, **Total Fat** 24 g, **Saturated Fat** 10 g, **Cholesterol** 100 mg, **Sodium** 910 mg, **Carbohydrate** 25 g, **Fiber** 2 g, **Protein** 34 g

U.S. Diabetic exchanges per serving: 1½ Starch, 4 Lean Meat, 2½ Fat (1½ Carb)

Spicy Three-Pepper Fettuccine with Turkey Sausage

28 minutes

Yield: 6 servings

Spice things up by serving fettuccine with a creamy peppery sauce.

1 lb (450 g) uncooked turkey sausage

4 cups (1 L) chicken stock

8 oz (250 g) uncooked fettuccine

½ medium red onion

1 jar (16 oz) yellow and red roasted bell peppers, drained

1 medium chipotle pepper in adobo sauce plus 1 tbsp (15 mL) adobo sauce

2 garlic cloves, peeled

¼ cup (50 mL) fresh basil leaves

8 oz (250 g) reduced-fat cream cheese (Neufchâtel), cubed

1. Cook sausage in **11-** or **12-in. (28-** or **30-cm) Skillet** over medium-high heat 7-8 minutes or until cooked through, breaking into crumbles using **Mix 'N Chop**. Drain, if necessary. Return sausage to Skillet.

2. Add stock to Skillet. Cover; bring to a boil over medium-high heat. Add fettuccine; cover and cook 10 minutes, stirring occasionally.

3. Meanwhile, process onion, bell and chipotle peppers, adobo sauce and garlic in **Manual Food Processor** until coarsely chopped. Thinly slice basil using **Chef's Knife**.

4. Stir pepper mixture into Skillet. Cook, covered, 3-5 minutes or until fettuccine is tender but still firm.

5. Reduce heat to low. Stir in cream cheese until incorporated. Cover and cook 2 minutes. Stir in basil and serve.

Cook's Tips:

If desired, a 16 oz (370 mL) jar of roasted red peppers can be substituted for the roasted yellow and red bell peppers.

This recipe is spicy! For a milder version, use mild turkey sausage, a small chipotle pepper and omit the added adobo sauce.

U.S. Nutrients per serving: **Calories** 400, **Total Fat** 18 g, **Saturated Fat** 5 g, **Cholesterol** 75 mg, **Sodium** 1190 mg, **Carbohydrate** 37 g, **Fiber** 2 g, **Protein** 26 g

U.S. Diabetic exchanges per serving: 2 Starch, 2 Vegetable, 2½ Med-Fat Meat, ½ Fat (2 Carb)

Asian BBQ Chicken Drumsticks

22 minutes

These saucy east-meets-west drumsticks mingle all-American BBQ sauce with flavorful Asian ingredients.

8	chicken drumsticks (about 5-7 oz/150-200 g each)
¼	tsp (1 mL) ground black pepper
1	lime
1	1-in. (2.5-cm) piece fresh gingerroot, peeled
¾	cup (175 mL) sweet barbecue sauce (see Cook's Tip)
2	tbsp (30 mL) orange marmalade
1	tbsp (15 mL) reduced-sodium soy sauce
2	garlic cloves, pressed
1	tsp (5 mL) Asian-style hot sauce, such as Sriracha (optional)
¼	cup (50 mL) fresh cilantro
	Toasted sesame seeds (optional)

1. Place drumsticks into **Deep Covered Baker**; season with pepper. Microwave, covered, on HIGH 5 minutes.

2. Move center drumsticks to ends of baker and outer drumsticks to center. Microwave, covered, on HIGH 3-5 minutes or until internal temperature reaches 165°F (74°C) in thickest part of drumstick.

3. Meanwhile, for sauce, juice lime using **Citrus Press** to measure 2 tsp (10 mL). Grate ginger using **Ginger Grater** to measure 2 tsp (10 mL).

4. Combine lime juice, ginger, barbecue sauce, marmalade, soy sauce, garlic pressed with **Garlic Press** and hot sauce, if desired, in **(1.5-qt./1.4-L) Saucepan**. Bring to a simmer over medium heat. Cook and stir 1 minute.

5. Carefully pour off juices from baker. Pour sauce over drumsticks; toss to coat using **Chef's Tongs**.

6. Microwave, covered, on HIGH 1-2 minutes or until heated through. Chop cilantro with **Santoku Knife**; sprinkle chicken with cilantro and sesame seeds, if desired.

Cook's Tips:

Use a basic sweet barbecue sauce for this recipe. Avoid sauces that are too spicy or smoky which might disturb the bold Asian flavors.

The sauce for this recipe can also be used on grilled chicken or fish!

U.S. Nutrients per serving: **Calories** 390, **Total Fat** 18 g, **Saturated Fat** 4.5 g, **Cholesterol** 175 mg, **Sodium** 980 mg, **Carbohydrate** 21 g, **Fiber** 1 g, **Protein** 34 g

U.S. Diabetic exchanges per serving: 1½ Fruit, 5 Lean Meat (1½ Carb)

Southwest Grilled Chicken Tortilla Salad

This fresh ingredient-packed salad served in a fun tortilla shell will be a family hit.

Yield: 6 servings

6   (8-in./20-cm) flour tortillas

1   lb (450 g) boneless, skinless chicken breasts

1   tbsp (15 mL) plus 2 tsp (10 mL) **Southwestern Seasoning Mix**, divided

¼   tsp (1 mL) salt

½   small head iceberg lettuce (about 3 cups/750 mL thinly sliced)

1   ear fresh corn, husks and silk removed

2   plum tomatoes

1   cup (250 mL) fresh cilantro

1   lime

½   cup (125 mL) ranch dressing

2   oz (60 g) queso fresco cheese

1   can (15.5 oz or 540 mL) black beans, drained and rinsed

1. Preheat oven to 350°F (180°C). Invert six (**1-cup/250-mL**) **Prep Bowls** onto **Cookie Sheet**; spray generously with canola oil using **Kitchen Spritzer**.

2. Top each bowl with one tortilla; spray with oil. Bake 15-17 minutes or until browned and crisp. Remove tortilla bowls from oven to **Stackable Cooling Rack** (see Cook's Tip).

3. Meanwhile, heat **Grill Pan** over medium heat 5 minutes. Season chicken with *1 tbsp (15 mL)* of the seasoning mix and salt.

4. Spray pan with oil. Add chicken to pan; top with **Grill Press** and cook 4-5 minutes per side or until internal temperature reaches 165°F (74°C).

5. Meanwhile, thinly slice lettuce. Remove kernels from corn using **Kernel Cutter**. Place lettuce and corn into large **Bamboo Fiber Bowl**.

6. Core and dice tomatoes and coarsely chop cilantro; add to bamboo bowl.

7. For dressing, juice lime to measure 1 tbsp (15 mL). Combine juice, ranch dressing and remaining 2 tsp (10 mL) seasoning mix in (**2-cup/500-mL**) **Prep Bowl**; mix well.

8. Dice chicken. Add chicken and beans to bamboo bowl; mix well. Crumble cheese with **Easy Release Cheese Crumbler**. Divide salad among tortilla bowls; serve with dressing and cheese.

Cook's Tips:

Queso fresco is a Mexican cheese served on salads, tacos and other Mexican dishes. If desired, shredded Monterey Jack or cheddar cheese can be substituted for queso fresco.

To easily remove the tortilla bowls from the prep bowls, grab the underside of the prep bowl with **Chef's Tongs**. While holding the prep bowl with tongs, gently twist tortilla bowl to loosen.

U.S. Nutrients per serving: **Calories** 390, **Total Fat** 16 g, **Saturated Fat** 3.5 g, **Cholesterol** 50 mg, **Sodium** 840 mg, **Carbohydrate** 36 g, **Fiber** 4 g, **Protein** 23 g

U.S. Diabetic exchanges per serving: 2½ Starch, 2 Lean Meat, 1½ Fat (2½ Carb)

Hazelnut-Crusted Turkey with Cannellini Salad

This colorful main dish salad brings simple turkey cutlets to an elegant new level.

Yield: 6 servings

Salad

- ½ cup (125 mL) sun-dried tomatoes (not oil-packed)
- 1 lemon
- 1 romaine lettuce heart (3 cups/750 mL thinly sliced)
- ¼ cup (50 mL) fresh parsley
- ¼ small red onion
- 1 can (15 oz or 398 mL) cannellini beans, drained and rinsed
- 2 tbsp (30 mL) olive oil
- ¼ tsp (1 mL) salt
- ½ tsp (2 mL) ground black pepper

Turkey

- 2 egg whites
- 1 cup (250 mL) whole hazelnuts
- ½ cup (125 mL) plain dry bread crumbs
- ¼ cup (50 mL) olive oil, divided
- 1 pkg (1.1 lbs or 450 g) turkey cutlets (see Cook's Tip)
- ½ tsp (2 mL) *each* salt and ground black pepper

1. For salad, thinly slice tomatoes using **Santoku Knife**. Combine tomatoes and ½ cup (125 mL) water in **Small Micro-Cooker®**. Microwave, covered, on HIGH 1-2 minutes or until softened. Drain and set aside.

2. Zest lemon using **Microplane® Zester** to measure 1 tsp (5 mL). Juice lemon to measure 1 tbsp (15 mL).

3. Thinly slice lettuce and chop parsley. Thinly slice onion using **Simple Slicer** on #1 setting. Combine tomatoes, zest, juice, lettuce, parsley, onion, beans, oil, salt and pepper in large **Bamboo Fiber Bowl**; mix well.

4. For turkey, beat egg whites until frothy in first **Coating Tray**. Finely process hazelnuts in **Manual Food Processor**. Add hazelnuts and bread crumbs to second tray; mix well.

5. Heat *2 tbsp (30 mL)* of the oil in **11-** or **12-in. (28-** or **30-cm) Skillet** over medium heat 1-3 minutes or until shimmering.

6. Season turkey with salt and pepper. Dip turkey into egg and then into hazelnut mixture, pressing firmly to coat.

7. Add half of the turkey to Skillet; cook 1-2 minutes per side or until golden brown. Wipe Skillet clean and repeat with remaining 2 tbsp (30 mL) oil and turkey. Serve turkey with salad.

Cook's Tips:

Turkey cutlets in a 1.1 lbs package can have 6-8 cutlets per package depending on the weight of the cutlets. If there are eight in a package, cut two of the cooked cutlets in thirds and serve 1½ pieces per serving.

Either blanched or unblanched hazelnuts will work in this recipe. If desired, slivered almonds can be substituted for the hazelnuts.

U.S. Nutrients per serving: **Calories** 400, **Total Fat** 24 g, **Saturated Fat** 2.5 g, **Cholesterol** 35 mg, **Sodium** 560 mg, **Carbohydrate** 18 g, **Fiber** 5 g, **Protein** 29 g

U.S. Diabetic exchanges per serving: 1 Starch, 3½ Med-Fat Meat, 1½ Fat (1 Carb)

White BBQ Pulled Chicken Pizza

28 minutes

Yield: 6 servings

A unique white BBQ sauce accents this out-of-the-ordinary pizza.

1 small pkg (6.5 oz) pizza crust mix

2 tsp (10 mL) canola oil

1 small rotisserie chicken (about 3 cups/750 mL shredded)

½ cup (125 mL) light mayonnaise

2 tbsp (30 mL) cider vinegar

1 tbsp (15 mL) prepared horseradish

2 tsp (10 mL) honey

¼ tsp (1 mL) ground black pepper

4 cups (1 L) baby spinach leaves

1 red apple such as Fuji or Jonathan

1½ cups (375 mL) shredded part-skim mozzarella cheese

1. Move oven rack to lowest position. Preheat oven to 450°F (230°C). Prepare pizza crust according to package directions. Knead dough on floured **Cutting Board** 1 minute or until dough is no longer sticky.

2. Brush **Large Round Stone with Handles** with oil. Place dough in center of stone and roll to an even thickness to edge of stone. Bake 10-12 minutes or until crust is golden brown.

3. Meanwhile, remove chicken from bones and shred. Combine mayonnaise, vinegar, horseradish, honey and pepper in **(2-cup/500-mL) Prep Bowl**; mix well. Set aside 2 tbsp (30 mL) of the sauce. Combine chicken and remaining sauce in **Classic Batter Bowl**; mix well.

4. Coarsely chop spinach using **Santoku Knife**. Core apple using **The Corer™**. Thinly slice apple using **Simple Slicer** on #2 setting. Stack apple slices and cut into thin strips.

5. Carefully remove stone from oven to **Stackable Cooling Rack**. Top crust evenly with cheese and chicken mixture. Return to oven and bake 2-3 minutes or until cheese is melted.

6. Meanwhile, combine spinach, apple and reserved sauce in medium **Bamboo Fiber Bowl**; toss to coat. Cut pizza into 12 slices; top with spinach mixture.

Cook's Tips:

If desired, you can substitute a 13.8 oz (283 g) package of refrigerated pizza dough for the pizza crust mix. To do so, skip Steps 1 and 2. Lightly brush Large Round Stone with Handles with oil. Unroll pizza dough onto stone. Roll dough to an even thickness to within ¼ in (1 cm) of edge of stone using **Baker's Roller®**. Bake 12-15 minutes or until crust is golden brown. Proceed as recipe directs.

U.S. Nutrients per serving (2 slices): **Calories** 390, **Total Fat** 16 g, **Saturated Fat** 5 g, **Cholesterol** 75 mg, **Sodium** 610 mg, **Carbohydrate** 32 g, **Fiber** 2 g, **Protein** 29 g

U.S. Diabetic exchanges per serving: 2 Starch, 2 Med-Fat Meat (2 Carb)

Cavatappi & Meatballs in Lemon-Basil Sauce

Yield: 6 servings

Hearty chicken meatballs and pasta make an easy and comforting dinner for any night of the week.

1. Cook pasta according to package directions. Drain and set aside.

2. Meanwhile, for meatballs, process onion, garlic and rub in **Manual Food Processor** until onion is finely chopped. Grate cheese with **Microplane® Adjustable Fine Grater**. Remove and discard crusts from bread; tear bread into pieces.

3. Combine bread, onion mixture, egg and cheese in **Stainless (4-qt./4-L) Mixing Bowl**; mix until a smooth paste forms. Add chicken and mix gently but thoroughly.

4. Heat oil in **11-** or **12-in. (28-** or **30-cm) Skillet** *(do not use stainless cookware)* over medium heat 1-3 minutes or until shimmering. Using a level **Medium Scoop**, scoop meat mixture, forming 24 meatballs, into Skillet. Cook, uncovered, 7-9 minutes or until golden brown, turning occasionally. Remove meatballs from Skillet.

5. To prepare sauce, juice lemon using **Juicer** to measure 1 tbsp (15 mL). Process juice, onion, garlic and rub in Manual Food Processor until onion is finely chopped.

6. Add oil and onion mixture to Skillet. Cook 1-2 minutes or until onion is softened. Add stock and wine; cook 2 minutes. Stir in cheese, salt and sugar.

7. Return meatballs to Skillet. Stir in pasta. Cook, covered, 2-3 minutes or until hot. Chop parsley. Sprinkle parsley over pasta.

Pasta & Meatballs

8	oz (250 g) uncooked cavatappi pasta
1	small yellow onion
2	garlic cloves, peeled
2½	tbsp (37 mL) **Sweet Basil Rub**
2	oz (60 g) fresh Parmesan cheese
2	slices white sandwich bread
1	egg, lightly beaten
1	lb (450 g) ground chicken
1½	tbsp (22 mL) olive oil

Sauce

1	lemon
1	small yellow onion
3	garlic cloves, peeled
½	tbsp (7 mL) Sweet Basil Rub
1	tbsp (15 mL) olive oil
1¼	cups (300 mL) chicken stock
½	cup (125 mL) dry white wine such as Sauvignon Blanc
¼	cup (50 mL) mascarpone cheese
½	tsp (2 mL) *each* salt and sugar
1	cup (250 mL) fresh parsley

Cook's Tips:

If desired, rotini or penne pasta can be substituted for the cavatappi.

If desired, 2 oz (60 g) of softened cream cheese can be substituted for the mascarpone.

If desired, 2 tbsp (30 mL) dried basil, 1 tsp (5 mL) sugar, 1 tsp (5 mL) paprika, ¾ tsp (4 mL) salt and ½ tsp (2 mL) ground black pepper can be substituted for the Sweet Basil Rub.

U.S. Nutrients per serving: **Calories** 450, **Total Fat** 21 g, **Saturated Fat** 7 g, **Cholesterol** 115 mg, **Sodium** 930 mg, **Carbohydrate** 37 g, **Fiber** 2 g, **Protein** 25 g

U.S. Diabetic exchanges per serving: 2½ Starch, 2½ Med-Fat Meat, 1 Fat (2½ Carb)

Tangy Lemon-Chicken Stir-Fry

28 minutes

Dry sherry is an unexpected ingredient that adds unique flavor in this simple stir-fry.

Jasmine rice
(optional, see Cook's Tip)

1-2	lemons
1	1-in. (2.5-cm) piece fresh gingerroot, peeled
4	green onions, divided
¼	cup (50 mL) reduced-sodium soy sauce
3	tbsp (45 mL) dry sherry (see Cook's Tip)
2	tbsp (30 mL) brown sugar
1	lb (450 g) boneless, skinless chicken thighs
8	oz (250 g) cremini mushrooms
1	tbsp (15 mL) canola oil
2	tsp (10 mL) cornstarch
1	cup (250 mL) broccoli florets

1. Begin cooking rice, if using (see Cook's Tip).

2. Zest lemon using **Zester/Scorer** to measure 2 tsp (10 mL); set aside. Juice lemon to measure 3 tbsp (45 mL). Grate ginger using **Ginger Grater** to measure 2 tsp (10 mL).

3. Thinly slice green onions; set aside 2 tbsp (30 mL) of the green tops for garnish. In **Classic Batter Bowl**, combine lemon juice, ginger, remaining green onions, soy sauce, sherry and brown sugar; mix well.

4. Cut chicken into 1-in. (2.5-cm) pieces; add to batter bowl and mix well. Cover and refrigerate 10 minutes.

5. Meanwhile, on a clean **Cutting Board**, cut mushrooms into quarters using **Paring Knife** and set aside.

6. Heat oil in **Stir-Fry Skillet** over medium-high heat 1-3 minutes or until shimmering. Place **(7-in./18-cm) Strainer** over **Small Batter Bowl**. Pour chicken into strainer allowing marinade to drain into batter bowl (do not discard marinade).

7. Add chicken to Skillet; cook 3-4 minutes or until browned on all sides, stirring occasionally. Whisk cornstarch into marinade.

8. Add mushrooms and broccoli to Skillet; cook and stir 3-4 minutes or until vegetables are crisp-tender.

9. Add marinade and zest to Skillet; bring to a simmer and cook 1-2 minutes or until sauce is thickened. Transfer stir-fry to a serving platter and garnish with reserved green onion tops. Serve with rice, if desired.

Cook's Tips:

For jasmine rice, combine 1 cup (250 mL) uncooked jasmine rice and 1½ cups (375 mL) water in **Rice Cooker Plus**. Microwave, covered, on HIGH for 10 minutes. Let stand covered for 10 minutes. Fluff with a fork and serve.

Dry sherry can be found in the liquor section of the grocery store. It has a clear color similar to white wine. Brands found on the bottom shelf are inexpensive and perfect for cooking. Avoid bottles labeled as "cooking sherry," which have added salt.

U.S. Nutrients per serving: **Calories** 240, **Total Fat** 8 g, **Saturated Fat** 1.5 g, **Cholesterol** 110 mg, **Sodium** 690 mg, **Carbohydrate** 15 g, **Fiber** 1 g, **Protein** 25 g

U.S. Diabetic exchanges per serving: ½ Fruit, 1 Vegetable, 4 Lean Meat (½ Carb)

Chicken Sausage Cassoulet

This quick version of a hearty French stew will surprise you with its simplicity.

1. Chop onion, celery and garlic using **Food Chopper**.

2. Slice bacon crosswise into ½-in. (1-cm) strips using **Santoku Knife**. Cook bacon in **(4-qt./3.8-L) Casserole** over medium-high heat 3 minutes, stirring occasionally.

3. Reduce heat to medium. Add onion, celery, garlic and *1 tsp (5 mL)* of the thyme to Casserole; cook 3-4 minutes or until vegetables are softened, stirring occasionally.

4. Add wine to Casserole; cook 1-2 minutes or until liquid is reduced by half.

5. Meanwhile, dice sausage into ½-in. (1-cm) pieces. Add sausage, beans, tomatoes, stock and pepper to Casserole; cover and bring to a simmer, stirring occasionally. Cook 3-5 minutes or until flavors are blended.

6. Meanwhile, mix panko, oil and remaining ½ tsp (2 mL) thyme in **Small Micro-Cooker®**. Microwave, covered, on HIGH 30-60 seconds or until toasted, stirring halfway through cooking. Ladle cassoulet into serving bowls; top with panko mixture.

1	medium onion
2	celery ribs
2	garlic cloves, peeled
4	slices uncooked bacon
1½	tsp (7 mL) dried thyme leaves, divided
½	cup (125 mL) dry white wine such as Sauvignon Blanc
12	oz (350 g) cooked chicken sausage (see Cook's Tip)
2	cans (15 oz/540 mL each) Great Northern beans, drained and rinsed
2	cans (14.5 oz/398 mL) fire-roasted diced tomatoes, undrained
1	cup (250 mL) chicken stock
¼	tsp (1 mL) ground black pepper
1	cup (250 mL) panko bread crumbs
2	tbsp (30 mL) olive oil

Cook's Tips:

Chicken sausage comes in a variety of flavors. For best results in this recipe, use a chicken sausage that has flavors such as tomatoes, herbs or even mushrooms. Avoid sausages with spicy flavors, such as jalapeño peppers.

If desired, regular canned diced tomatoes can be substituted for the fire-roasted tomatoes.

U.S. Nutrients per serving (1⅓ cups/325 mL): **Calories** 390, **Total Fat** 18 g, **Saturated Fat** 5 g, **Cholesterol** 55 mg, **Sodium** 1150 mg, **Carbohydrate** 30 g, **Fiber** 8 g, **Protein** 20 g

U.S. Diabetic exchanges per serving: 1½ Starch, 1 Vegetable, 2 High-Fat Meat, 1 Fat (1½ Carb)

Chicken & Apricot Curry

Sweet apricots with fresh ginger and Indian curry make magic in the microwave in this surprising curry dish.

28 minutes

1 cup (250 mL) uncooked basmati rice

1 lb (450 g) boneless, skinless chicken thighs

1 medium onion

2 tbsp (30 mL) **Indian Mild Curry Rub**

2 cups (500 mL) chicken stock

1 2-in. (5-cm) piece fresh gingerroot, peeled

½ cup (125 mL) plain full-fat Greek yogurt (see Cook's Tip)

2 tbsp (30 mL) cornstarch

½ tsp (2 mL) salt

1½ cups (375 mL) dried apricots

2 green onions

Toasted slivered almonds (optional)

1. Rinse rice under warm running water 1 minute in **(7-in./18-cm) Strainer**, gently shaking to remove excess starch.

2. Combine rice and 2 cups (500 mL) water in **(3-qt./2.8-L) Saucepan**. Cover; bring to boil. Reduce heat to low; cook 10 minutes. Remove Saucepan from heat and let stand, covered, 5 minutes. Fluff rice with fork.

3. Meanwhile, dice chicken into ½-in. (1-cm) pieces using **Chef's Knife**. Chop onion using **Food Chopper**.

4. Add chicken, onion and rub to **Deep Covered Baker**; mix well. Microwave, covered, on HIGH 5-6 minutes or until chicken is mostly cooked through, stirring once.

5. Meanwhile, bring stock to a boil in **(1.5-qt./1.4-L) Saucepan**.

6. Grate ginger using **Ginger Grater** to measure 2 tbsp (30 mL). Combine ginger, yogurt, cornstarch and salt in **Classic Batter Bowl**; whisk well. Slowly pour stock into yogurt mixture, whisking vigorously until combined.

7. Cut apricots into quarters. Add stock mixture and apricots to baker; mix well. Cover and microwave on HIGH 8-10 minutes or until curry is hot and thickened.

8. Thinly slice green onions. Carefully remove baker from microwave using **Microwave Grips**. Serve curry with rice; sprinkle with green onions and almonds, if desired.

Cook's Tips:

If desired, 1½ tbsp (22 mL) curry powder and 1 tsp (5 mL) salt can be substituted for the Indian Mild Curry Rub.

Greek yogurt is thicker than regular yogurt and lends a creamy texture to this dish. Be sure to use a full-fat Greek yogurt for this recipe, or the sauce will break. Look for a Greek yogurt that contains at least 9 grams of fat per serving.

To toast almonds, place ⅓ cup (75 mL) slivered almonds into **Small Micro-Cooker®**. Cover and microwave on HIGH 1-2 minutes or until toasted, stirring every 30 seconds.

U.S. Nutrients per serving: **Calories** 320, **Total Fat** 8 g, **Saturated Fat** 3.5 g, **Cholesterol** 115 mg, **Sodium** 950 mg, **Carbohydrate** 35 g, **Fiber** 4 g, **Protein** 28 g

U.S. Diabetic exchanges per serving: 1½ Starch, 1 Fruit, 3 Lean Meat (2½ Carb)

Smoky Cheddar-Stuffed Turkey Sliders

You'll love the smoky flavor in these all-American cheesy sliders topped with a tempting sauce.

3   green onions, divided
2½   tbsp (37 mL)
       Smoky Red Pepper Rub
3   garlic cloves, peeled
½   tsp (2 mL) ground
       black pepper
1   lb (450 g) 93% lean
       ground turkey
3   oz (90 g) sharp white
       cheddar cheese
½   tbsp (7 mL) canola oil
⅓   cup (75 mL) mayonnaise
2-3   plum tomatoes
12   small Bibb lettuce leaves
12   soft dinner rolls or slider
       mini buns

1. Cut green tops off of onions and set aside. Process white bottoms of onions, rub, garlic and pepper in **Manual Food Processor** until finely chopped.

2. Combine onion mixture and turkey in **Classic Batter Bowl**; mix gently but thoroughly.

3. Cut cheese into ½-in. (1-cm) cubes. Using rounded **Medium Scoop**, divide turkey mixture evenly into 12 balls. Place one cheese cube into each ball and form patty around cheese, sealing edges so cheese is no longer visible.

4. Heat oil in **(12-in./30-cm) Skillet** over medium heat 1-3 minutes or until shimmering. Cook patties 2-3 minutes per side or until internal temperature reaches 165°F (74°C).

5. Meanwhile, for sauce, process green onion tops in Manual Food Processor until finely chopped. Add mayonnaise; process until combined.

6. Slice tomatoes into 12 slices. To serve, place lettuce, tomatoes and patties on bun bottoms; top with sauce and bun tops.

Cook's Tips:

If desired, regular sharp cheddar cheese can be substituted for the white cheddar.

To make this recipe in a **(11-in./28-cm) Skillet**, cook the patties in two batches, dividing the oil.

U.S. Nutrients per serving: **Calories** 420, **Total Fat** 19 g, **Saturated Fat** 5 g, **Cholesterol** 65 mg, **Sodium** 650 mg, **Carbohydrate** 39 g, **Fiber** 3 g, **Protein** 27 g

U.S. Diabetic exchanges per serving: 2½ Starch, 3 Med-Fat Meat (2½ Carb)

Lemon Pepper Chicken & Crispy Potatoes

This easy dinner will put your mind at ease when it comes to doing dishes; the chicken, potatoes and sauce are all made in the same Skillet!

Yield: 4 servings

3   small russet potatoes (about 5 oz/150 g each)

4   boneless, skinless chicken breasts (about 5-6 oz/ 150-175 g each)

2   tbsp (30 mL) **Lemon Pepper Rub**

2   tbsp (30 mL) olive oil, divided

¼   cup (50 mL) butter (½ stick)

1   lemon

¼   tsp (1 mL) salt

¼   tsp (1 mL) ground black pepper

½   cup (125 mL) chicken stock

2   garlic cloves, pressed
     Chopped fresh parsley (optional)

1. Cut potatoes into wedges using **Veggie Wedger**. Place potatoes and enough water to cover into **Large Micro-Cooker®**; microwave, covered, on HIGH 9-11 minutes or until potatoes are tender. Drain and set aside.

2. Meanwhile, gently flatten chicken to ½-in. (1-cm) thickness using flat side of **Meat Tenderizer**. Season chicken with rub.

3. Heat 1 tbsp (15 mL) of the oil in **11-** or **12-in. (28-** or **30-cm) Skillet** *(do not use stainless cookware)* over medium heat 1-3 minutes or until shimmering. Add chicken; cook 4-4½ minutes per side or until internal temperature reaches 165°F (74°C). Remove chicken from Skillet; set aside and keep warm.

4. Meanwhile, dice butter into ½-in. (1-cm) cubes and juice lemon using **Juicer** to measure 1 tsp (5 mL); set aside.

5. In a clean Skillet, heat remaining 1 tbsp (15 mL) oil over medium heat 1-3 minutes or until shimmering. Add potatoes, cut side down to Skillet. Sprinkle with salt and pepper; cook 2-3 minutes per side or until golden brown. Remove potatoes from Skillet; set aside.

6. For sauce, add stock, garlic pressed with **Garlic Press**, butter and lemon juice to Skillet; whisk using **Silicone Flat Whisk** until butter is incorporated. Bring to a simmer; cook an additional 30-60 seconds or until slightly thickened, stirring occasionally.

7. Serve chicken with potatoes and sauce. Sprinkle with parsley, if desired.

Cook's Tips:

To clean the Skillet before Step 5, grab two folded paper towels with tongs and wipe the Skillet clean.

If desired, any lemon pepper seasoning can be substituted for the Lemon Pepper Rub.

U.S. Nutrients per serving: **Calories** 400, **Total Fat** 22 g, **Saturated Fat** 9 g, **Cholesterol** 110 mg, **Sodium** 820 mg, **Carbohydrate** 20 g, **Fiber** 1 g, **Protein** 32 g

U.S. Diabetic exchanges per serving: 1 Starch, 4 Lean Meat, 2 Fat (1 Carb)

Thai Peanut
Chicken Noodle Salad

Creamy peanut butter combined with bright vegetables–perfect for introducing kids to Thai flavors.

Yield: 4 servings

8	oz (250 g) uncooked angel hair pasta
½	cup (125 mL) creamy peanut butter
3	tbsp (45 mL) rice vinegar
2	tbsp (30 mL) soy sauce
2	tbsp (30 mL) water
4	tsp (20 mL) Thai red curry paste
1	medium red bell pepper
¼	seedless cucumber
3	green onions, divided
1	cup (250 mL) dry-roasted, salted peanuts
1	cup (250 mL) fresh cilantro
8	chicken tenders (1 lb/450 g)

1. Cook pasta according to package directions. Drain and rinse under cold water.

2. Meanwhile, for sauce, combine peanut butter, vinegar, soy sauce, water and curry paste in **Stainless (4-qt./4-L) Mixing Bowl**; whisk well. Set aside ¼ cup (50 mL) of the sauce in **Classic Batter Bowl**.

3. For salad, coarsely chop bell pepper using **Food Chopper**.

4. Slice cucumber lengthwise into quarters, then crosswise into ¼-inch-thick (6-mm) slices. Thinly slice green onions. Set aside 2 tbsp (30 mL) of the green tops for garnish.

5. Add bell pepper, cucumber, remaining green onions and pasta to stainless mixing bowl. Mix well using **Chef's Tongs**.

6. Heat **Grill Pan** over medium heat 5 minutes. Finely chop peanuts and cilantro using Food Chopper. Place peanuts and cilantro into **Coating Tray**; mix well.

7. Spray pan with canola oil using **Kitchen Spritzer**. Add chicken to pan; top with **Grill Press** and cook 3-5 minutes or until internal temperature reaches 165°F (74°C), turning once.

8. Remove chicken from pan and add to reserved sauce in batter bowl; toss to coat. Press chicken into peanut mixture. Serve chicken with salad; garnish with reserved green onion tops.

Cook's Tips:

Thai curry paste is a blend of chilies, garlic, shallots, lemongrass and other Thai flavors. It can also be used for any type of stir-fry or Asian-style soup. Thai green curry paste is also available but is generally spicier.

If desired, boneless, skinless chicken breasts can be substituted for the chicken tenders. Slice the breasts lengthwise into strips and proceed as directed.

U.S. Nutrients per serving: **Calories** 730, **Total Fat** 36 g, **Saturated Fat** 7 g, **Cholesterol** 65 mg, **Sodium** 1020 mg, **Carbohydrate** 59 g, **Fiber** 8 g, **Protein** 48 g

U.S. Diabetic exchanges per serving: 1½ Starch, 2 Fruit, 1 Vegetable, 6 High-Fat Meat (3½ Carb)

Turkey Meatloaf "Cupcakes"

28 minutes

Yield: 6 servings

The "wow" about these tender meatloaves is that they're prepared in the microwave!

1½ cups (375 mL) refrigerated prepared mashed potatoes

2 tbsp (30 mL) sour cream

2 oz (60 g) sharp cheddar cheese

¼ cup (50 mL) plus 2 tbsp (30 mL) plain dry bread crumbs, divided

½ cup (125 mL) fresh parsley, divided

2 shallots

1½ lbs (700 g) 93% lean ground turkey

½ cup (125 mL) chili sauce

1 whole egg plus 1 egg yolk

½ tsp (2 mL) *each* salt and ground black pepper

1. Place potatoes into **Classic Batter Bowl**. Cover loosely with lid and microwave on HIGH 2-3 minutes or until hot. Stir in sour cream. Set aside.

2. Meanwhile, cut cheese into 6 cubes; set aside. Spray wells of **Single Servings Pan** with canola oil using **Kitchen Spritzer**. Coat wells with *2 tbsp (30 mL)* of the bread crumbs; set aside.

3. Finely chop parsley and shallots using **Food Chopper**. Set aside *1 tbsp (15 mL)* of the parsley for garnish.

4. Combine remaining parsley, shallots, turkey, chili sauce, egg, egg yolk, salt, pepper and remaining ¼ cup (50 mL) bread crumbs in large **Bamboo Fiber Bowl**; mix well.

5. On **Flexible Cutting Mat**, divide turkey mixture into 6 mounds using **Large Scoop** (about three level scoops per mound). Place one cheese cube into center of each mound and form into a ball. Place mounds into wells of pan, pressing tops to flatten and pressing cheese cube to the bottom.

6. Microwave, uncovered, on HIGH 7-9 minutes or until tops are firm and internal temperature in the sides of each meatloaf reaches 165°F (74°C).

7. Remove pan from microwave; let stand 2 minutes. Carefully lift meatloaves from wells using releasing tool. Using clean, level Large Scoop, scoop potatoes over meatloaves; garnish with reserved parsley.

Cook's Tips:

Warming the potatoes *first* gives the potatoes time to cool slightly, making them easier to top the meatloaves.

To absorb excess moisture, lightly blot the sides of the meatloaves with paper towels before topping with potatoes.

To make this recipe without using a microwave, preheat oven to 350°F (180°C). Heat potatoes according to package directions. Stir in sour cream; cover and set aside. Prepare meatloaves as directed through Step 5. Bake 24-26 minutes or until tops are firm and internal temperature in the sides of each loaf reaches 165°F (74°C).

U.S. Nutrients per serving: **Calories** 350, **Total Fat** 16 g, **Saturated Fat** 7 g, **Cholesterol** 150 mg, **Sodium** 920 mg, **Carbohydrate** 22 g, **Fiber** 1 g, **Protein** 28 g

U.S. Diabetic exchanges per serving: 1½ Starch, 3 Med-Fat Meat, 1 Fat (1½ Carb)

Crab Louie Lettuce Wraps p. 63

Tilapia with Kale & Brown Butter Dressing p. 49

Cornmeal Crusted Cod with Spicy Ketchup p. 61

Jamaican Coconut Shrimp p. 57

fish & seafood
DISHES

Make a splash at the dinner table with family-friendly fish and seafood plates.

Sautéed Halibut with Arugula Salad

The delicate flavor of halibut is complemented by peppery arugula and tangy vinaigrette.

24 minutes

Yield: 4 servings

3   medium oranges, divided
3   tbsp (45 mL) white
       wine vinegar
2   tbsp (30 mL) orange
       marmalade
3   tbsp (45 mL) **Sweet Basil
       Rub**, divided
¼   cup (50 mL) canola
       oil, divided
½   small red onion
1   avocado
4   skinless, fresh or frozen,
       thawed halibut fillets
       (4-6 oz/125-175 g each),
       patted dry
1   pkg (5 oz) fresh arugula
       (about 6 cups/1.5 L)

1. Zest one of the oranges using **Microplane® Zester** to measure 1 tbsp (15 mL) and juice to measure 2 tsp (10 mL). Cut remaining two oranges into segments using **Paring Knife** (see Cook's Tip). Set orange segments aside.

2. For dressing, combine zest, juice, vinegar, marmalade and *1 tbsp (15 mL)* of the rub in **Small Batter Bowl**; whisk well. Slowly add *2 tbsp (30 mL)* of the oil while whisking.

3. Thinly slice onion and dice avocado using **Santoku Knife**.

4. Heat remaining 2 tbsp (30 mL) oil in **(10-in./24-cm) Skillet** over medium-high heat 1-3 minutes or until shimmering. Season halibut with remaining 2 tbsp (30 mL) rub.

5. Add halibut to Skillet; reduce heat to medium and cook 2-3 minutes per side or until halibut flakes easily with a fork.

6. Meanwhile, set aside ¼ cup (50 mL) of the dressing to serve with halibut. In **Stainless (4-qt./4-L) Mixing Bowl**, gently toss arugula with remaining dressing, orange segments, onion and avocado.

7. Drizzle halibut with reserved dressing and serve with salad.

Cook's Tips:

To cut orange into segments, cut a ½-in. (1-cm) slice from top and bottom of the orange. Rest orange on one of its flat cut sides; cutting from top to bottom, trim away the entire peel and white membrane, exposing the flesh. Cut along the membrane on the left and right side of each orange segment. Angle the knife under each segment and lift out.

If desired, 2 tbsp (30 mL) dried basil, 1 tsp (5 mL) sugar, 1 tsp (5 mL) paprika, ¾ tsp (4 mL) salt and ½ tsp (2 mL) ground black pepper can be substituted for the Sweet Basil Rub.

U.S. Nutrients per serving: **Calories** 370, **Total Fat** 23 g, **Saturated Fat** 2.5 g, **Cholesterol** 55 mg, **Sodium** 680 mg, **Carbohydrate** 21 g, **Fiber** 6 g, **Protein** 23 g

U.S. Diabetic exchanges per serving: 1½ Fruit, 3 Med-Fat Meat, 2 Fat (1½ Carb)

Savory Shrimp Rolls

Yield: 4 servings

Dig in to a tempting east coast favorite that calls for shrimp instead of lobster.

1 lb (450 g) large uncooked shrimp (21-25 per pound), peeled, deveined and tails removed

2 tbsp (30 mL) **Chive & Tarragon Seasoning Mix**, divided

2 garlic cloves, pressed

1 tbsp (15 mL) olive oil

1 lemon

2 tbsp (30 mL) light mayonnaise

1 tbsp (15 mL) Dijon mustard

2 tsp (10 mL) honey

4 (6-7-in./15-18-cm) hoagie rolls, uncut

1 celery rib

2 plum tomatoes

2 green onions

1. Preheat oven to 400°F (200°C). Combine shrimp, *1 tbsp (15 mL)* of the seasoning mix and pressed garlic in small **Bamboo Fiber Bowl**; mix well.

2. Heat oil in **(10-in./24-cm) Sauté Pan** over medium-high heat 1-3 minutes or until shimmering. Add shrimp; cook 3-4 minutes or until browned and cooked through. Remove shrimp from pan. Set aside.

3. Meanwhile, juice lemon to measure 1 tbsp (15 mL). Combine lemon juice, mayonnaise, mustard, honey and remaining 1 tbsp (15 mL) seasoning mix in **Classic Batter Bowl**; mix well.

4. Slice each roll lengthwise, leaving ½ in. (1 cm) on each end. Gently pull apart rolls and spread open to create a pocket. Spray rolls with olive oil using **Kitchen Spritzer**. Place on **Medium Sheet Pan**. Bake 5-7 minutes or until crisp.

5. Chop celery using **Food Chopper**. Core and seed tomatoes using **Core & More**. Dice tomatoes and thinly slice green onions using **Chef's Knife**.

6. Coarsely chop shrimp. Add shrimp, celery, tomatoes and green onions to batter bowl; mix well. Scoop salad into rolls using **Medium Scoop** and serve.

Cook's Tips:

If purchasing shrimp with shells on, account for the shell waste and purchase an additional ¼ lb (125 g) shrimp to make the total amount used equal 1 lb (450 g).

The shrimp salad portion of this recipe can be made and refrigerated up to 1 hour in advance.

U.S. Nutrients per serving: **Calories** 270, **Total Fat** 9 g, **Saturated Fat** 1.5 g, **Cholesterol** 145 mg, **Sodium** 980 mg, **Carbohydrate** 27 g, **Fiber** 2 g, **Protein** 19 g

U.S. Diabetic exchanges per serving: 2 Starch, 2 Lean Meat (2 Carb)

Spaghetti with Fresh Tomato Clam Sauce

Yield: 6 servings

Bring everyone to the table with this fresh Italian-inspired meal.

12   oz (350 g) uncooked thin spaghetti
3   shallots
6   garlic cloves, peeled
2   tbsp (30 mL) olive oil
½   tsp (2 mL) crushed red pepper flakes
1   cup (250 mL) dry white wine such as Chardonnay
2   pints grape tomatoes
3   cans (6.5 oz each) chopped clams in juice, undrained (2¾ cups/675 mL)
2   tbsp (30 mL) butter
1½   cups (375 mL) fresh parsley

1. Cook spaghetti according to package directions (see Cook's Tip). Drain and set aside.

2. Process shallots and garlic in **Manual Food Processor** until finely chopped.

3. Add shallot mixture, oil and crushed red pepper flakes to **11-** or **12-in. (28-** or **30-cm) Skillet**. Cook over medium-high heat 2-3 minutes or until fragrant, stirring occasionally.

4. Add wine and tomatoes to Skillet; cover and bring to a simmer. Cook 3-4 minutes or until tomatoes begin to soften. Mash tomatoes using **Mix 'N Masher**.

5. Add clams and butter to Skillet. Cover; return to a simmer and cook 3 minutes or until flavors are well blended. Chop parsley using **Chef's Knife**.

6. Add spaghetti to Skillet. Continue cooking and mixing spaghetti with **Chef's Tongs** for 1 minute. Remove Skillet from heat and mix in parsley. Serve immediately.

Cook's Tips:

Adding a generous amount of salt to the water seasons pasta while cooking it and eliminates the need to add additional salt to the sauce. To cook the pasta in this recipe, bring 10 cups (2.4 L) of water and 2 tbsp (30 mL) of salt to a boil in **(4.75-qt./4.5-L) Casserole**. Add the pasta and cook according to timing on package, stirring occasionally. Drain, but do not rinse. Proceed as recipe directs. *(Nutritionals do not reflect added salt to pasta water.)*

Parsley is used for both color and flavor in this recipe. For best results, use parsley labeled as "flat-leaf" or "Italian" parsley. It has larger leaves than its curly cousin and has more flavor.

U.S. Nutrients per serving: **Calories** 380, **Total Fat** 9 g, **Saturated Fat** 3.5 g, **Cholesterol** 25 mg, **Sodium** 650 mg, **Carbohydrate** 53 g, **Fiber** 3 g, **Protein** 16 g

U.S. Diabetic exchanges per serving: 3 Starch, 2 Vegetable, ½ Lean Meat, 1 Fat (3 Carb)

Tilapia with Kale
& Brown Butter Dressing

The brown butter in the dressing adds a nutty flavor to this quick and easy meal.

4   tilapia fillets (1 lb/450 g)

¾   tsp (4 mL) salt, divided

½   tsp (2 mL) ground black pepper, divided

2   tbsp (30 mL) olive oil

½   cup (125 mL) flour

1   bunch fresh kale (about 8 cups/2 L chopped)

2   shallots

3   tbsp (45 mL) water

¼   cup (50 mL) butter (½ stick)

1   tbsp (15 mL) Dijon mustard

1   tbsp (15 mL) white wine vinegar

1   tsp (5 mL) honey

1. Cut each fillet into three pieces (see Cook's Tip). Season with ½ tsp (2 mL) of the salt and ¼ tsp (1 mL) of the pepper.

2. Heat oil in **11-** or **12-in. (28-** or **30-cm) Skillet** over medium-high heat 1-3 minutes or until shimmering.

3. Place flour into **Coating Tray**. Dredge tilapia in flour, shaking off excess.

4. Add tilapia to Skillet; cook 3-4 minutes per side or until golden brown and tilapia flakes easily with a fork. Remove tilapia from Skillet; tent with foil to keep warm.

5. Meanwhile, remove and discard stems from kale (see Cook's Tip); coarsely chop leaves using **Chef's Knife**. Finely chop shallots using **Food Chopper**.

6. Add kale, shallots, water and remaining ¼ tsp (1 mL) *each* salt and pepper to Skillet; cook 60-90 seconds or until kale is tender, stirring constantly. Remove kale from Skillet to **Classic Batter Bowl**.

7. Add butter to Skillet; cook 60-90 seconds or until butter turns an amber color and gives off a nutty aroma. (Watch carefully so butter does not burn.) Transfer butter to **(1-cup/250-mL) Easy Read Measuring Cup**.

8. For dressing, add mustard, vinegar and honey to **Small Batter Bowl**. Slowly add butter to batter bowl, whisking vigorously. Serve tilapia with kale and dressing.

Cook's Tips:

To cut tilapia into three equal pieces, slice the fillet down the center into two portions. Cut the thicker portion on an angle into two pieces. This will ensure even cooking.

To chop kale, cut along the stem to remove the leafy green parts. Discard stems. Stack leaves; cut lengthwise into strips, then cut crosswise.

U.S. Nutrients per serving: **Calories** 360, **Total Fat** 21 g, **Saturated Fat** 9 g, **Cholesterol** 85 mg, **Sodium** 740 mg, **Carbohydrate** 19 g, **Fiber** 3 g, **Protein** 28 g

U.S. Diabetic exchanges per serving: ½ Starch, 2 Vegetable, 3 Lean Meat (½ Carb)

California Niçoise Salad Toss

Enhance pasta and canned tuna, two pantry staples, with fresh vegetables for a bright and colorful dish.

8   oz (250 g) uncooked penne pasta

3   tbsp (45 mL) country Dijon or brown mustard

1   tbsp (15 mL) red wine vinegar

1   tbsp (15 mL) honey

½   tsp (2 mL) ground black pepper

1   tbsp (15 mL) canola oil

4   oz (125 g) fresh green beans

1   vine-ripened tomato

½   pkg (¾ oz/20 g) fresh chives (⅓ cup/75 mL coarsely chopped)

1   jar (6.5 oz or 170 mL) marinated artichokes, drained

½   cup (125 mL) pitted kalamata olives

1   small avocado

2   cans (5 oz or 170 g each) solid white albacore tuna, in water, drained

    Butter lettuce leaves (optional)

1. Cook pasta according to package directions. Drain and set aside.

2. Meanwhile for dressing, combine mustard, vinegar, honey and pepper in **Small Batter Bowl**; whisk well. Slowly add oil while whisking. Set aside.

3. Trim and slice green beans using **Bean Slicer**. Place green beans and enough water to cover in **Large Micro-Cooker®**. Microwave, covered, on HIGH 2-3 minutes or until crisp-tender. Drain and fill Micro-Cooker® with ice water; set aside.

4. Coarsely chop tomato and chives using **Chef's Knife**. Coarsely chop artichokes using **Food Chopper**.

5. Cut olives in half lengthwise. Peel and dice avocado.

6. Drain green beans. Combine green beans, pasta, dressing, tomato, chives, artichokes, olives and tuna in large **Bamboo Fiber Bowl**; mix well.

7. Line **Round Serving Bowl** with lettuce leaves, if desired. Transfer salad to serving bowl and top with avocado.

Cook's Tips:

If you don't have the Bean Slicer, lay green beans 3 or 4 at a time on **Cutting Board** and thinly slice crosswise on a bias. Proceed as directed in Step 3.

Do not use oil-packed tuna for this recipe as it could make the salad more oily than desired.

U.S. Nutrients per serving: **Calories** 510, **Total Fat** 19 g, **Saturated Fat** 2.5 g, **Cholesterol** 25 mg, **Sodium** 890 mg, **Carbohydrate** 62 g, **Fiber** 8 g, **Protein** 26 g

U.S. Diabetic exchanges per serving: 3 Starch, 3 Vegetable, 2 Lean Meat, 2 Fat (3 Carb)

Chunky Shrimp Verde Chowder

Bold flavors like cumin, poblano pepper and tomatillo salsa are the key to getting great quick flavor in this recipe.

Yield: 6 servings
(9 cups/2.1 L)

1   medium onion
1   jalapeño pepper
1   cup (250 mL) fresh cilantro
3   garlic cloves, peeled
1   tbsp (15 mL) canola oil
1   tsp (5 mL) ground cumin
1   poblano pepper
1   large red potato (8 oz/250 g)
3   cups (750 mL) chicken broth
1   jar (16 oz) tomatillo salsa
     (1¾ cups/425 mL)
1   lb (450 g) large uncooked
     shrimp (21-25 per pound),
     peeled, deveined and
     tails removed
1   cup (250 mL) frozen corn
     kernels
1   avocado

1. Cut onion into quarters. Cut jalapeño lengthwise in half and remove seeds using **Core & More**. Process onion, jalapeño, cilantro and garlic in **Manual Food Processor** until finely chopped.

2. Add onion mixture, oil and cumin to **(4-qt./3.8-L) Casserole**. Cook over medium heat 3-4 minutes or until onion is softened.

3. Meanwhile, dice poblano and potato into ½-in. (1-cm) pieces. Add poblano to Casserole; cook 1-2 minutes or until poblano begins to soften.

4. Place potato and enough water to cover into **Small Micro-Cooker®**. Microwave, covered, on HIGH 5-6 minutes or until potato is tender. Drain and set aside.

5. Add broth and salsa to Casserole. Bring to a simmer and cook 5 minutes.

6. Cut shrimp in half. Add shrimp, potato and corn to Casserole; cook 2-3 minutes or until shrimp are cooked through.

7. Peel and dice avocado using **Avocado Peeler**. Transfer chowder to serving bowls and top with avocado.

Cook's Tips:

A small green bell pepper can be substituted for the poblano, if desired.

Use the **French Fry Cutter** to quickly cut the potato lengthwise into strips, then dice the potato strips crosswise into ½-in. (1-cm) pieces.

U.S. Nutrients per serving (1½ cups/375 mL): **Calories** 210, **Total Fat** 9 g, **Saturated Fat** 1 g, **Cholesterol** 95 mg, **Sodium** 1180 mg, **Carbohydrate** 22 g, **Fiber** 5 g, **Protein** 15 g

U.S. Diabetic exchanges per serving: 1 Starch, 1½ Vegetable, 1 Lean Meat, 1 Fat (1 Carb)

Dijon Salmon Burgers

Give beef a break and try these juicy burgers made with fresh salmon.

½   small red bell pepper

1   shallot

¼   cup (50 mL) fresh parsley

1   lemon

1   lb (450 g) skinless salmon fillet

½   cup (125 mL) panko bread crumbs

1   egg

2   tbsp (30 mL) **Dijon Mustard Rub**, divided

¾   tsp (4 mL) salt

¼   tsp (1 mL) ground black pepper

¼   cup (50 mL) sour cream

2   tbsp (30 mL) mayonnaise

½   tsp (2 mL) honey

4   multi grain or whole grain buns

1   tbsp (15 mL) canola oil

4   green leaf lettuce leaves

1. Preheat oven to 425°F (220°C). Process bell pepper, shallot and parsley in **Manual Food Processor** until finely chopped. Transfer bell pepper mixture to large **Bamboo Fiber Bowl**.

2. Juice lemon using **Juicer** to measure 2 tbsp (30 mL). Dice salmon into ½-in. (1-cm) pieces.

3. Add half of the salmon and half of the juice to Manual Food Processor; process until finely chopped. Transfer to bamboo bowl with bell pepper mixture. Repeat with remaining salmon and juice.

4. Add panko, egg, *1 tbsp (15 mL)* of the rub, salt and black pepper to bamboo bowl; mix well.

5. For sauce, combine sour cream, mayonnaise, honey and remaining 1 tbsp (15 mL) rub in **(2-cup/500-mL) Prep Bowl**; mix well.

6. Place buns, cut side up onto **Large Sheet Pan**. Bake 7-8 minutes or until toasted.

7. Form salmon mixture into four ¾-inch-thick (2-cm) patties. Heat oil in **(12-in./30-cm) Skillet** over medium-high heat 1-3 minutes or until shimmering. Add patties; cook 3 minutes per side or until golden brown.

8. Remove buns from oven. Place lettuce on bun bottoms; top with burgers, sauce and bun tops.

Cook's Tips:

Be sure not to over-process the salmon in this recipe. The chunks of salmon give the patties a nice texture and prevent them from becoming chewy.

If desired, these patties can be formed several hours ahead of time. Place formed patties on **Flexible Cutting Mat**; wrap in plastic and refrigerate.

To make this recipe in a **(11-in./28-cm) Skillet**, cook the patties in two batches, dividing the oil.

U.S. Nutrients per serving: **Calories** 540, **Total Fat** 30 g, **Saturated Fat** 6 g, **Cholesterol** 120 mg, **Sodium** 850 mg, **Carbohydrate** 30 g, **Fiber** 3 g, **Protein** 30 g

U.S. Diabetic exchanges per serving: 2 Starch, 3½ Med-Fat Meat, 2½ Fat (2 Carb)

Jamaican Coconut Shrimp

Yield: 4 servings

How do you get your kids to eat shrimp? Coat it in crispy coconut and serve it with pineapple-studded rice!

1   cup (250 mL) converted long grain rice

¾   tsp (4 mL) salt

½   tsp (2 mL) ground black pepper

16   extra large shrimp (16-20 per pound), peeled, deveined and tails intact

2   tbsp (30 mL) **Jamaican Jerk Rub**

2   tbsp (30 mL) cornstarch

2   egg whites

1½   cups (375 mL) sweetened flaked coconut

¼   cup (50 mL) canola oil

½   cup (125 mL) fresh cilantro, divided

½   small red bell pepper

1   can (8 oz) pineapple tidbits, drained (about ½ cup/125 mL)

1. For pineapple rice, combine rice, 2 cups (500 mL) water, salt and black pepper in **Rice Cooker Plus**. Microwave, covered, on HIGH 14-16 minutes or until rice is cooked. Let stand 5 minutes.

2. Meanwhile, using tip of **Paring Knife**, cut each shrimp down the back, from neck to tail, almost all the way through. Ease open with fingers.

3. Combine shrimp and rub in large **Bamboo Fiber Bowl**; mix well to coat.

4. Add cornstarch to bamboo bowl; mix well. Beat egg whites until frothy and add to bamboo bowl; mix until thoroughly combined.

5. Place coconut into **Coating Tray**. Press and lightly flatten shrimp into coconut, coating evenly.

6. Heat oil in **11-** or **12-in. (28-** or **30-cm) Skillet** (*do not use stainless cookware*) over medium heat 1-3 minutes or until shimmering.

7. Add shrimp to Skillet. Cook 2-3 minutes per side or until golden brown.

8. Meanwhile, chop cilantro; set aside 1 tbsp (15 mL) for garnish. Chop bell pepper using **Food Chopper**.

9. Add remaining cilantro, bell pepper and pineapple to rice; mix well. Serve shrimp with pineapple rice and sprinkle with reserved cilantro.

Cook's Tips:

If desired, any jerk or Caribbean seasoning can be substituted for the Jamaican Jerk Rub.

Coating the shrimp in cornstarch rather than flour helps the egg stick to the shrimp better, which in turn allows the coconut to adhere more easily.

U.S. Nutrients per serving: **Calories** 570, **Total Fat** 24 g, **Saturated Fat** 10 g, **Cholesterol** 145 mg, **Sodium** 1500 mg, **Carbohydrate** 66 g, **Fiber** 4 g, **Protein** 23 g

U.S. Diabetic exchanges per serving: 3 Starch, 1½ Fruit, 2 Lean Meat, 3 Fat (4½ Carb)

Ricotta Crêpes
with Smoked Salmon

29 minutes

Yield: 4 servings

Ricotta cheese provides an unexpected tenderness to smoked salmon-filled crêpes.

1. To prepare crêpes, zest lemon to measure 2 tsp (10 mL). Juice lemon to measure 1 tbsp (15 mL); set aside for use in sauce. Combine zest and remaining crêpe ingredients in blender; blend until smooth.

2. Spray **(8-in./20-cm) Sauté Pan** *(do not use stainless cookware)* with canola oil using **Kitchen Spritzer**. Heat over medium heat 1-3 minutes or until shimmering.

3. Pour ⅓ cup (75 mL) batter into pan. When crêpe starts to bubble and edges are brown, turn over using **Small Nylon Turner**. Cook additional 1 minute or until lightly browned (see Cook's Tip).

4. Repeat with remaining batter, lightly spraying pan with additional oil after every other crêpe for a total of eight crêpes.

5. For sauce, whisk cream cheese, milk, dill mix, lemon juice and salt in **(2-cup/500-mL) Prep Bowl** until smooth.

6. Slice onion half using **Simple Slicer** on #1 setting; cut slices in half. Cut tomatoes in half.

7. To assemble, spread 1 tbsp (15 mL) of the sauce over each crêpe; top evenly with capers, onion, tomatoes and salmon. Fold crêpes and dollop with remaining sauce.

Crêpes

1   lemon
3   eggs
1   cup (250 mL) milk
¾   cup (175 mL) flour
⅔   cup (150 mL) part-skim ricotta cheese
1   tsp (5 mL) baking powder
¼   tsp (1 mL) salt

Sauce & Filling

6   oz (175 g) reduced-fat cream cheese (Neufchâtel), softened
½   cup (125 mL) milk
1   tbsp (15 mL) **All-Purpose Dill Mix**
1   tbsp (15 mL) lemon juice (from lemon used in crêpes)
⅛   tsp (0.5 mL) salt
½   small red onion
1   cup (250 mL) grape tomatoes
2   tbsp (30 mL) capers, drained and rinsed
4   oz (125 g) cold-smoked salmon, thinly sliced (see Cook's Tip)

Cook's Tips:

Cold-smoked salmon is cured in a mixture of salt, sugar and spices. It is sold sliced paper thin and can be found in a vacuum pack in the fish department of most major grocery stores. Be sure to look for cold-smoked salmon as opposed to lox or gravlax, which are not smoked.

Because of the delicate nature of the batter, if crêpes begin to brown too quickly, turn down the heat to medium-low.

U.S. Nutrients per serving (2 crêpes): **Calories** 400, **Total Fat** 20 g, **Saturated Fat** 10 g, **Cholesterol** 200 mg, **Sodium** 980 mg, **Carbohydrate** 29 g, **Fiber** 1 g, **Protein** 24 g

U.S. Diabetic exchanges per serving: 2 Starch, 2½ Med-Fat Meat, 1 Fat (2 Carb)

Cornmeal Crusted Cod with Spicy Ketchup

Yield: 4 servings

A quick cornmeal coating and a kick of spice make fish a family favorite!

½   small onion

1   jalapeño pepper

1   garlic clove, peeled

1   lime

¼   cup (50 mL) canola oil, divided

⅓   cup (75 mL) ketchup

1½   tbsp (22 mL) brown sugar

4   tsp (20 mL) chili powder, divided

¼   cup (50 mL) flour

2   egg whites

½   cup (125 mL) yellow cornmeal

4   fresh or frozen, thawed cod fillets (4-6 oz/125-175 g each)

½   tsp (2 mL) salt

¼   tsp (1 mL) ground black pepper

1. For spicy ketchup, chop onion, jalapeño and garlic using **Food Chopper**. Juice lime using **Citrus Press** to measure 1 tbsp (15 mL).

2. Heat *½ tbsp (7 mL)* of the oil in **(1.5-qt./1.4-L) Saucepan** over medium-high heat 1-3 minutes or until shimmering. Add onion, jalapeño and garlic to Saucepan. Cook 2-3 minutes or until onion is softened, stirring often.

3. Reduce heat to low; stir in ketchup, brown sugar and *1 tsp (5 mL)* of the chili powder; cook 1 minute. Remove Saucepan from heat; stir in lime juice and set aside.

4. Place flour into first **Coating Tray**. Lightly beat egg whites in second tray. Combine cornmeal and remaining 3 tsp (15 mL) chili powder in third tray.

5. Season cod with salt and black pepper. Lightly dredge cod in flour, shaking off excess. Dip into egg whites and then into cornmeal mixture, pressing firmly to coat.

6. Heat remaining 3½ tbsp (52 mL) oil in **11-** or **12-in. (28-** or **30-cm) Skillet** over medium-high heat 1-3 minutes or until shimmering. Add cod; cook 2-4 minutes or until golden brown. Reduce heat to medium; carefully turn cod over using **Small Nylon Turner**. Cook 2-3 minutes or until golden brown and cod flakes easily with a fork. Serve with spicy ketchup.

Cook's Tips:

For a milder spicy ketchup, remove the seeds from the jalapeño before preparing.

Using egg whites instead of whole eggs to coat the cod makes for a crisper coating.

U.S. Nutrients per serving: **Calories** 380, **Total Fat** 16 g, **Saturated Fat** 1.5 g, **Cholesterol** 50 mg, **Sodium** 650 mg, **Carbohydrate** 35 g, **Fiber** 2 g, **Protein** 25 g

U.S. Diabetic exchanges per serving: 1½ Starch, 1 Fruit, 3 Lean Meat, 1 Fat (2½ Carb)

Crab Louie Lettuce Wraps

Yield: 4 servings

These fun lettuce leaf-wrapped bites will appeal to even the pickiest eater.

1. Slice cucumber with **Simple Slicer** on #3 setting; cut slices into quarters. Snip chives.

2. Combine cucumber, chives, crabmeat and capers in **Classic Batter Bowl**; stir gently. Finely dice roasted red peppers; gently fold into crab mixture.

3. For sauce, juice lemon using **Juicer** to measure 1 tbsp (15 mL). Mix juice, mayonnaise, chili sauce, Worcestershire and cayenne pepper in **(2-cup/500-mL) Prep Bowl** until blended.

4. Gently stir sauce into crab mixture; spoon crab salad into lettuce leaves.

- ½ seedless cucumber
- ¼ cup (50 mL) snipped fresh chives
- 2 cans (6.5 oz or 175 g each) lump crabmeat, drained (see Cook's Tip)
- 2 tbsp (30 mL) capers, drained and rinsed
- ¼ cup (50 mL) jarred roasted red peppers, drained and patted dry
- 1 lemon
- ⅓ cup (75 mL) light mayonnaise
- 1 tbsp (15 mL) chili sauce
- 1 tsp (5 mL) Worcestershire sauce
- ¼ tsp (1 mL) cayenne pepper
- 8 Bibb lettuce leaves

Cook's Tips:

When draining, press down on crabmeat with paper towels to remove excess moisture.

If desired, romaine lettuce leaves can be substituted for the Bibb lettuce.

U.S. Nutrients per serving (2 wraps): **Calories** 140, **Total Fat** 8 g, **Saturated Fat** 1 g, **Cholesterol** 90 mg, **Sodium** 1100 mg, **Carbohydrate** 8 g, **Fiber** 1 g, **Protein** 13 g

U.S. Diabetic exchanges per serving: ½ Vegetable, 2 Lean Meat, ½ Fat (0 Carb)

Easy 'N Cheesy Pasta Bake p. 85

Buffalo Blue Cheese Steaks & Fries p. 83

Spicy Thin-Crust Sausage Pizza p. 77

Gravy-Smothered Sausage Burgers p. 99

beef & pork DISHES

Feed the family hearty beef and pork dishes; they'll never know they're quick-cooking!

Japanese Steakhouse Pork Chops

Yield: 4 servings

These outstanding pork chops are glazed with a mouth watering Japanese-style sauce and wasabi mashed potatoes.

Pork & Sauce

4	bone-in pork chops, cut ¾ in. (2 cm) thick (6 oz/175 g each)
½	cup (125 mL) reduced-sodium soy sauce, divided
½	cup (125 mL) water, divided
3	garlic cloves, pressed
2	tbsp (30 mL) honey
2	tsp (10 mL) cornstarch
1	1-in. (2.5-cm) piece fresh gingerroot, peeled
1	tsp (5 mL) wasabi paste

Potatoes

1	lb (450 g) small yellow potatoes
8	garlic cloves, peeled
½	cup (125 mL) milk
2	tbsp (30 mL) butter
1	tsp (5 mL) wasabi paste
¼	tsp (1 mL) salt

1. Prick pork several times using **Hold 'N Slice®**. Combine pork, ¼ *cup (50 mL) each* of the soy sauce, water and pressed garlic in a large resealable plastic bag; turn to coat. Refrigerate until ready to use.

2. Cut potatoes into 1-in. (2.5-cm) cubes. Place potatoes, garlic and enough water to cover in **Large Micro-Cooker®**. Microwave, covered, on HIGH 12-14 minutes or until potatoes are tender; drain.

3. Add remaining potato ingredients and mash with **Mix 'N Masher**. Cover and set aside.

4. As potatoes cook, heat **Grill Pan** over medium-high heat 5 minutes.

5. For sauce, whisk remaining ¼ cup (50 mL) *each* soy sauce and water, honey and cornstarch in **Small Micro-Cooker®**. Microwave, uncovered, on HIGH 1-2 minutes or until mixture is boiling and thick.

6. Grate ginger using **Ginger Grater** to measure 1 tsp (5 mL). Add ginger and wasabi paste to sauce mixture.

7. Remove pork from marinade; discard marinade. Spray pan with olive oil using **Kitchen Spritzer**. Add pork to pan; top with **Grill Press**. Cook 4-6 minutes per side or until internal temperature of pork reaches 145°F (63°C). Serve pork with potatoes and sauce.

Cook's Tips:

Wasabi is Japanese horseradish that is typically served with sushi. It is spicy and has a pungent aroma. Wasabi paste comes in a tube and can be found in the Asian section of the grocery store.

Cooking the whole garlic cloves with the potatoes and mashing them gives the mashed potatoes a sweeter, milder garlic flavor compared to adding raw garlic.

U.S. Nutrients per serving: **Calories** 450, **Total Fat** 14 g, **Saturated Fat** 6 g, **Cholesterol** 135 mg, **Sodium** 1180 mg, **Carbohydrate** 38 g, **Fiber** 3 g, **Protein** 43 g

U.S. Diabetic exchanges per serving: 1½ Starch, 1 Fruit, 5½ Lean Meat (2½ Carb)

Easy Beef Stew
with Parmesan Polenta

Create a quick-cooking stew with fresh herbs, veggies and flavorful tender steak.

Yield: 6 servings

1   tbsp (15 mL) olive oil

1¼   lbs (575 g) boneless top sirloin or New York strip steak, trimmed

½   tsp (2 mL) *each* salt and ground black pepper

2   medium onions

2   garlic cloves, pressed

2   cans (14 oz each) beef broth (about 4 cups/1 L), divided

⅓   cup (75 mL) flour

3   stems *each* fresh rosemary and thyme

1   cup (250 mL) dry red wine such as Cabernet Sauvignon

1½   cups (375 mL) frozen mixed peas and carrots

     Parmesan Polenta
     (see Cook's Tip)

1. Preheat oven to 400°F (200°C). Heat oil in pan of **Covered Roaster** over medium-high heat 1-3 minutes or until shimmering.

2. Cut steak into 1-in. (2.5-cm) cubes and place in **Classic Batter Bowl**. Add salt and pepper; mix well. Transfer steak to Roaster pan; cook 4-5 minutes or until browned, stirring once. Remove steak from pan; set aside.

3. Meanwhile, chop onions using **Food Chopper**. Add onions and garlic pressed with **Garlic Press** to pan; cook 2-3 minutes or until onions are softened.

4. Whisk together ½ cup (125 mL) of the broth and flour in **(2-cup/500-mL) Prep Bowl** until flour has dissolved.

5. Place herbs into **Herb Infuser**. Add remaining 3½ cups (875 mL) broth, Herb Infuser and wine to pan; bring to a boil.

6. Reduce heat to medium and whisk in flour mixture using **Silicone Sauce Whisk**. Simmer 10 minutes.

7. Meanwhile, prepare *Parmesan Polenta* (see Cook's Tip).

8. Add steak and frozen vegetables to pan; return to a simmer 5 minutes. Using **Chef's Tongs**, remove Herb Infuser from pan. Serve stew with *Parmesan Polenta*.

Cook's Tips:

To ensure the flour mixture is fully incorporated, whisk it again just before whisking into stew.

For *Parmesan Polenta*, whisk together 3 cups (750 mL) hot water, 1 cup (250 mL) instant polenta and ½ tsp (2 mL) *each* salt and ground black pepper in **Large Micro-Cooker®**. Microwave, covered, on HIGH 2-3 minutes or until thick, stirring halfway through cooking. Stir in ¼ cup (50 mL) butter and 1 cup (250 mL) grated fresh Parmesan cheese. Add 1 egg and mix vigorously until incorporated. Spread mixture evenly into lid of Covered Roaster; bake 9-10 minutes or until **Pocket Thermometer** registers 160°F (71°C) when inserted into center.

U.S. Nutrients per serving: **Calories** 440, **Total Fat** 17 g, **Saturated Fat** 8 g, **Cholesterol** 105 mg, **Sodium** 1200 mg, **Carbohydrate** 36 g, **Fiber** 3 g, **Protein** 28 g

U.S. Diabetic exchanges per serving: 2½ Starch, 3 Med-Fat Meat (2½ Carb)

Bacon, Leek & Potato Hash with Eggs

26 minutes

Yield: 4 servings

A combination of bacon and smoked paprika puts this satisfying egg dish above the rest!

4   slices uncooked bacon

½   lb (250 g) Yukon gold potatoes

½   medium red bell pepper

1   small leek

½   tsp (2 mL) smoked paprika

¼   tsp (1 mL) *each* salt and ground black pepper

3   oz (90 g) reduced-fat cream cheese (Neufchâtel), softened

6   eggs

1½   oz (45 g) shredded white cheddar cheese, divided

     Chopped fresh parsley (optional)

1. Thinly slice bacon crosswise into ¼-in. (6-mm) strips. Cook bacon in **(10-in./24-cm) Skillet** over medium-high heat 6-7 minutes or until crisp, stirring occasionally. Remove bacon from Skillet (do not discard drippings).

2. Meanwhile, dice potatoes. Place potatoes and enough water to cover into **Large Micro-Cooker®**. Microwave, covered, on HIGH 3-4 minutes or until almost tender; drain.

3. Dice bell pepper using **Chef's Knife**. Cut leek in half lengthwise, then crosswise into strips. Place into **Classic Batter Bowl** and rinse with cold water; drain.

4. Add 2 tsp (10 mL) of the bacon drippings, potatoes, bell pepper, leek, paprika, salt and black pepper to Skillet. Cook and stir 5-6 minutes, adding bacon during last minute of cook time. Remove hash from Skillet.

5. Meanwhile, whisk cream cheese until smooth in **Small Batter Bowl**. Add eggs; whisk well (see Cook's Tip).

6. Heat an additional 2 tsp (10 mL) bacon drippings in a clean Skillet over medium-high heat.

7. Add egg mixture to Skillet; cook 30 seconds or until egg is set around sides. Pull egg from sides using **Classic Scraper** and tilt Skillet to allow egg to flow underneath; continue cooking 1-2 minutes or until mostly set.

8. Sprinkle egg mixture with *half* of the cheese. Reduce heat to low; cover and cook 1-2 minutes or until set and cheese is melted. Cut egg into wedges; serve with hash and sprinkle with remaining cheese and parsley, if desired.

Cook's Tips:

Use the **French Fry Cutter** to easily cut the potatoes into strips. Place the strips on **Cutting Board** and dice.

To avoid lumps in the egg mixture, microwave the cream cheese, uncovered, on HIGH for 30-60 seconds, then whisk until smooth. Add one egg and whisk vigorously. Add salt, pepper and remaining eggs and whisk again until smooth.

U.S. Nutrients per serving: **Calories** 350, **Total Fat** 23 g, **Saturated Fat** 10 g, **Cholesterol** 320 mg, **Sodium** 590 mg, **Carbohydrate** 15 g, **Fiber** 2 g, **Protein** 19 g

U.S. Diabetic exchanges per serving: 1 Starch, 2 Med-Fat Meat, 2½ Fat (1 Carb)

Pork Pot Sticker Stir-Fry

25 minutes

Yield: 6 servings

Using prepared pot stickers is a fun way to get a restaurant-style stir-fry in no time!

1½ tbsp (22 mL) canola oil

24 frozen pork and vegetable pot stickers (about 1 lb/450 g)

4 green onions

½ medium red bell pepper

2 carrots

1 1-in. (2.5-cm) piece fresh gingerroot

8 oz (250 g) ground pork

2 garlic cloves, pressed

8 oz (250 g) sugar snap peas, trimmed (see Cook's Tip)

1 can (8.75 oz) whole baby sweet corn, drained (about 1 cup/250 mL)

¼ cup (50 mL) reduced-sodium soy sauce

2 tsp (10 mL) toasted sesame oil

1 tsp (5 mL) cornstarch

1. Heat canola oil over medium-high heat in **11-** or **12-in. (28-** or **30-cm) Skillet** *(do not use stainless cookware)* 1-3 minutes or until shimmering. Add pot stickers; cook 6-8 minutes or until golden brown, stirring frequently. Remove from Skillet.

2. Meanwhile, thinly slice green onions and dice bell pepper with **Santoku Knife**. Cut carrots into julienne strips using **Julienne Peeler**. Grate ginger using **Ginger Grater** to measure 1 tsp (5 mL).

3. Add onions, ginger, pork and pressed garlic to Skillet. Cook over medium heat 3-4 minutes or until pork is cooked through, breaking into crumbles using **Mix 'N Chop**. Drain, if necessary, and return pork mixture to Skillet.

4. Add bell pepper, carrots, snap peas and baby corn to Skillet. Cook 3-4 minutes or until crisp-tender, stirring occasionally.

5. Mix soy sauce, sesame oil and cornstarch in **(1-cup/250-mL) Easy Read Measuring Cup**. Pour into Skillet; stir 1 minute or until heated through.

6. Return pot stickers to Skillet. Cook and stir 1 minute to heat through.

Cook's Tips:

Sugar snap peas have a small thin string on the inside edge that is best to remove before eating. To remove, pull off the ends and pull away.

The **Sauté Tongs** are the perfect tool for moving the pot stickers around the Skillet.

U.S. Nutrients per serving: **Calories** 300, **Total Fat** 15 g, **Saturated Fat** 3.5 g, **Cholesterol** 40 mg, **Sodium** 790 mg, **Carbohydrate** 25 g, **Fiber** 3 g, **Protein** 16 g

U.S. Diabetic exchanges per serving: 1½ Starch, ½ Vegetable, 1½ Med-Fat Meat, 1½ Fat (1½ Carb)

Steak Fajita Burritos

Switch it up by serving a fajita as an easy-to-eat wrap.

1 pkg (8 oz or 215 g) uncooked Mexican rice

2½ cups (625 mL) water

2 tbsp (30 mL) canola oil, divided

1 lb (450 g) skirt steak

2 tbsp (30 mL) **Tex-Mex Rub**

½ medium red bell pepper

½ medium yellow bell pepper

½ medium red onion

2 garlic cloves, pressed

¼ cup (50 mL) fresh cilantro

½ cup (125 mL) sour cream

1 cup (250 mL) shredded Chihuahua cheese

3 (11-in./28-cm) flour tortillas (see Cook's Tip)

1. Combine contents of rice package, water and *1 tbsp (15 mL)* of the oil in **Rice Cooker Plus**. Microwave, covered, on HIGH 18-20 minutes or until rice is cooked; set aside.

2. Pound steak using toothed side of **Meat Tenderizer**. Cut steak crosswise into thin strips (see Cook's Tip). Combine steak and rub in **Classic Batter Bowl**; mix well.

3. Heat remaining 1 tbsp (15 mL) oil in **11-** or **12-in. (28- or 30-cm) Skillet** over medium-high heat 1-3 minutes or until shimmering. Add steak; cook, undisturbed, 4-5 minutes or until browned on one side.

4. Meanwhile, thinly slice bell peppers and onion. Add vegetables to Skillet; cook 3-4 minutes or until vegetables are crisp-tender, stirring occasionally. Stir in garlic pressed with **Garlic Press** and remove Skillet from heat.

5. For sauce, chop cilantro. Combine cilantro and sour cream in **(1-cup/250-mL) Prep Bowl**.

6. To assemble burritos, sprinkle ⅓ cup (75 mL) of the cheese down center of one tortilla. Top with 1 cup (250 mL) of the rice, one-third of the steak mixture and one-third of the sauce. Fold in ends of tortillas and roll up tightly. Repeat with remaining ingredients. Cut burritos in half.

Cook's Tips:

Skirt steak should always be sliced against the grain, or it can be tough. The grain of the meat is the direction the fibers of the muscle run. By cutting the strip of meat into short sections, you can easily slice against the grain for the most tender results.

Warming the tortillas will make them easier to roll up. To warm tortillas, place them between paper towels and microwave on HIGH 30–45 seconds or until warm.

When placing the steak mixture over the rice, use **Chef's Tongs** to squeeze out any excess moisture to prevent the filling from being soggy.

U.S. Nutrients per serving (½ burrito): **Calories** 440, **Total Fat** 26 g, **Saturated Fat** 11 g, **Cholesterol** 75 mg, **Sodium** 770 mg, **Carbohydrate** 27 g, **Fiber** 1 g, **Protein** 24 g

U.S. Diabetic exchanges per serving: 2 Starch, 2½ Med-Fat Meat, 2 Fat (2 Carb)

Spicy Thin-Crust Sausage Pizza

27 minutes

Make homemade pizza in less time than it takes for delivery!

1 tbsp (15 mL) olive oil

1 pkg (11 oz) refrigerated thin-crust pizza crust

8 oz (250 g) uncooked hot Italian sausage

1 can (8 oz or 213 mL) tomato sauce

2 garlic cloves, pressed

½ tsp (2 mL) ground black pepper

1 cup (250 mL) fresh basil leaves

2 plum tomatoes

1 oz (30 g) fresh Parmesan cheese

2 cups (500 mL) shredded part-skim mozzarella cheese

Additional ground black pepper (optional)

1. Preheat oven to 450°F (230°C). Brush **Stoneware Cookie Sheet** with oil. Unroll pizza crust onto Cookie Sheet and roll up handles using **Baker's Roller®**. Prick dough all over with pastry tool. Bake on center rack of oven 15-17 minutes or until golden brown on top (see Cook's Tip).

2. Meanwhile, cook sausage in **(10-in./24-cm) Skillet** over medium-high heat 6-8 minutes or until cooked through, breaking into crumbles using **Mix 'N Chop**.

3. Add tomato sauce, garlic pressed with **Garlic Press** and pepper to Skillet. Bring to a simmer; cook 1-2 minutes or until sauce is absorbed into sausage.

4. Coarsely chop basil and seed and dice tomatoes using **Chef's Knife**. Set aside.

5. Grate Parmesan cheese using **Rotary Grater**. Combine cheeses in **(2-cup/500-mL) Prep Bowl**.

6. Loosen crust from Cookie Sheet using **Mega Lifter**. Top crust with half of the cheeses. Add sausage mixture and sprinkle with remaining cheeses. Bake 1-2 minutes or until cheeses are melted.

7. Cut pizza into 16 squares using **Pizza Cutter**. Sprinkle with basil, tomatoes and additional black pepper, if desired.

Cook's Tips:

The key to a crispy crust is making sure the dough stays adhered to the stone during baking, so keep an eye on it as it bakes! If you see pockets of the crust bubble up during baking, carefully pop them with a small knife.

Loosening the crust from the stone with the Mega Lifter allows air to get under the crust so it dries a little more, helping it get crisp. It also ensures the individual squares are easier to serve.

U.S. Nutrients per serving (2 squares): **Calories** 290, **Total Fat** 15 g, **Saturated Fat** 6 g, **Cholesterol** 25 mg, **Sodium** 790 mg, **Carbohydrate** 23 g, **Fiber** 1 g, **Protein** 15 g

U.S. Diabetic exchanges per serving: 1½ Starch, 1½ Med-Fat Meat, 1½ Fat (1½ Carb)

Crispy Crusted Pork with Tomato Jam

The rich flavor of pork medallions coated with butter-flavored crackers pairs perfectly with a tart tomato jam.

28 minutes

Yield: 6 servings

Jam

1	small yellow onion
6	garlic cloves, pressed
2	cups (500 mL) cherry tomatoes
3	tbsp (45 mL) red wine vinegar
2	tbsp (30 mL) brown sugar
1	tbsp (15 mL) olive oil
½	tsp (2 mL) *each* salt and ground black pepper

Pork

1½	lbs (700 g) pork tenderloin
2	eggs
30	butter-flavored crackers
1	tbsp (15 mL) **Crushed Peppercorn & Garlic Rub**
2	tbsp (30 mL) canola oil

1. For jam, process onion in **Manual Food Processor** until finely chopped.

2. Combine onion, garlic pressed with **Garlic Press** and remaining jam ingredients in **Large Micro-Cooker®**. Microwave, uncovered, on HIGH 12 minutes; cool 5 minutes.

3. Meanwhile, trim fat and silver skin from pork. Slice pork crosswise into ¾-in. (2-cm) slices.

4. Lightly beat eggs in first **Coating Tray**. Process crackers in clean Manual Food Processor until finely crushed. Combine cracker crumbs and rub in second tray.

5. Dip pork into eggs and then into crumb mixture, pressing firmly to coat.

6. Heat oil in **(12-in./30-cm) Skillet** over medium heat 1-3 minutes or until shimmering.

7. Add pork and cook 2-3 minutes per side or until golden brown and internal temperature of pork reaches 145°F (63°C). Remove pork from Skillet.

8. Process jam mixture in Manual Food Processor until finely chopped. Serve pork with jam.

Cook's Tips:

To make this recipe in a **(11-in./28-cm) Skillet**, cook the pork in two batches, dividing the oil.

Serve any leftover jam with roasted or grilled chicken or seafood.

U.S. Nutrients per serving: **Calories** 330, **Total Fat** 15 g, **Saturated Fat** 3 g, **Cholesterol** 135 mg, **Sodium** 700 mg, **Carbohydrate** 20 g, **Fiber** 1 g, **Protein** 28 g

U.S. Diabetic exchanges per serving: 1 Starch, 1 Vegetable, 3 Med-Fat Meat (1 Carb)

Beefy Mac & Cheese Soup

This hearty soup is quintessential comfort food that comes together in a snap!

26 minutes

Yield: 6 servings
(8 cups/2 L)

1. Melt butter in **(4-qt./3.8-L) Casserole** over medium heat. Stir in flour and black pepper; cook 1 minute.

2. Whisk milk and stock into Casserole. Cover and bring to a simmer, stirring occasionally.

3. Meanwhile, chop onion and bell pepper using **Food Chopper**. Set bell pepper aside.

4. Combine onion and beef in **Small Batter Bowl**. Microwave, uncovered, on HIGH 3-4 minutes or until cooked through, breaking into crumbles halfway through cooking using **Mix 'N Chop**. Drain and set aside.

5. Add noodles to Casserole. Return to a simmer and cook 9-10 minutes or until noodles are tender, stirring occasionally.

6. Meanwhile, dice American cheese using **Santoku Knife**. Add cheeses to Casserole; stir until melted.

7. Add bell pepper, beef mixture and corn to Casserole; return to a simmer. Cook 1-2 minutes or until heated through, stirring occasionally.

3	tbsp (45 mL) butter
3	tbsp (45 mL) flour
¼	tsp (1 mL) ground black pepper
3	cups (750 mL) milk
2	cups (500 mL) chicken stock
½	medium onion
½	medium red bell pepper
½	lb (225 g) 95% lean ground beef
1	cup (250 mL) uncooked elbow macaroni noodles
4	oz (125 g) pasteurized processed American cheese (about 6 slices)
1	cup (250 mL) shredded sharp cheddar cheese
1	cup (250 mL) frozen corn

Cook's Tips:

When adding noodles in Step 5, starches can cause slight bubble up. Use the small **Boil Over No More** to prevent potential spill over.

After chopping, squeeze the bell pepper between paper towels to get rid of excess moisture. This will prevent the soup from turning pink.

U.S. Nutrients per serving (about 1⅓ cups/325 mL): **Calories** 520, **Total Fat** 32 g, **Saturated Fat** 18 g, **Cholesterol** 120 mg, **Sodium** 1000 mg, **Carbohydrate** 28 g, **Fiber** 2 g, **Protein** 31 g

U.S. Diabetic exchanges per serving: 2 Starch, 3 Med-Fat Meat, 3 Fat (2 Carb)

Buffalo Blue Cheese Steaks & Fries

A homemade spicy butter is the secret to these tasty steaks and fries.

Yield: 4 servings

2 cups (500 mL) frozen French fries (about 8 oz/250 g)

1 cup (250 mL) fresh parsley

4 tbsp (60 mL) butter (½ stick), softened

1 tbsp (15 mL) **Buffalo Rub**

¼ cup (50 mL) crumbled blue cheese

4 boneless rib-eye steaks, cut ½ in. (1 cm) thick (6-8 oz/175-250 g each)

¼ tsp (1 mL) *each* salt and ground black pepper

1. Preheat oven to 450°F (230°C). Arrange fries on **Large Round Stone with Handles**. Bake 22-25 minutes or until golden brown.

2. Meanwhile process parsley, butter and rub in **Manual Food Processor** until parsley is finely chopped. Add blue cheese; process until blended.

3. Heat **Grill Pan** over medium-high heat 5 minutes. Sprinkle steaks with salt and pepper. Cook steaks 2-3 minutes per side or until internal temperature reaches 140°F (60°C) for medium-rare doneness.

4. Remove steaks from pan to **Cutting Board**; top each steak with 1 tbsp (15 mL) of the butter mixture. Tent with foil and let stand 5 minutes (temperature will rise to 145°F/63°C).

5. Remove fries from oven; place in **Stainless (2-qt./2-L) Mixing Bowl**. Immediately add remaining butter mixture to fries; toss using **Chef's Tongs** until coated. Serve with steaks.

Cook's Tips:

This spicy compound butter is perfect for other grilled meats like chicken, fish or even shrimp! If desired, double the butter recipe and roll up the remaining butter in **Parchment Paper**. Place reserved butter in the freezer until ready to use.

Never eat grilled steak right off the grill! Tenting the meat with foil and allowing it to rest causes the fibers in the meat to relax and brings out the natural juices.

U.S. Nutrients per serving: **Calories** 500, **Total Fat** 30 g, **Saturated Fat** 15 g, **Cholesterol** 135 mg, **Sodium** 790 mg, **Carbohydrate** 16 g, **Fiber** 2 g, **Protein** 37 g

U.S. Diabetic exchanges per serving: 1 Starch, 5 Med-Fat Meat, 1 Fat (1 Carb)

Easy 'N Cheesy Pasta Bake

24 minutes

Yield: 8 servings

Traditional pasta and meat sauce is transformed into baked squares topped with melty cheese.

8	oz (250 g) uncooked angel hair pasta
1	medium onion
2	tsp (10 mL) olive oil
12	oz (350 g) 90% lean ground beef
1	can (15 oz or 398 mL) tomato sauce
3	tbsp (45 mL) **Fennel & Herb Rub**, divided
¾	cup (175 mL) half and half
1	egg
½	tsp (2 mL) ground black pepper
¼	tsp (1 mL) salt
1	oz (30 g) fresh Parmesan cheese
1	cup (250 mL) shredded mozzarella cheese
	Chopped fresh parsley (optional)

1. Break pasta in half. Place pasta and 3 cups (750 mL) water in **Deep Covered Baker**. Microwave, covered, on HIGH 8-10 minutes or until pasta is tender.

2. Meanwhile, for meat sauce, finely chop onion using **Food Chopper**. Add onion and oil to **(10-in./24-cm) Skillet**. Cook over medium-high heat 3-4 minutes or until onion is softened, stirring occasionally.

3. Add beef to Skillet; cook 3-4 minutes or until beef is no longer pink, breaking into crumbles using **Mix 'N Chop**.

4. Add tomato sauce and *1½ tbsp (22 mL)* of the rub to Skillet. Bring to a simmer; reduce heat to medium-low and cook 2 minutes. Remove Skillet from heat; set aside.

5. Carefully remove baker from microwave using **Silicone Oven Mitts**. (Drain pasta if necessary.)

6. Combine half and half, egg, pepper, salt and remaining 1½ tbsp (22 mL) rub in **Small Batter Bowl**. Whisk until smooth.

7. Pour half and half mixture over pasta in baker; toss to coat using **Chef's Tongs**. Microwave, covered, on HIGH 3-4 minutes or until **Pocket Thermometer** registers 160°F (71°C) in center and pasta mixture is set.

8. Grate Parmesan cheese using **Rotary Grater**. Combine cheeses in **(2-cup/500-mL) Prep Bowl**; mix well.

9. Spread meat sauce over pasta mixture; sprinkle with cheeses. Cover; microwave on HIGH 1-2 minutes or until cheeses are melted. Sprinkle with parsley, if desired.

Cook's Tip:

If desired, 93% lean ground turkey can be substituted for the ground beef.

U.S. Nutrients per serving: **Calories** 300, **Total Fat** 13 g, **Saturated Fat** 6 g, **Cholesterol** 70 mg, **Sodium** 690 mg, **Carbohydrate** 27 g, **Fiber** 2 g, **Protein** 20 g

U.S. Diabetic exchanges per serving: 2 Starch, 2 Med-Fat Meat (2 Carb)

Middle Eastern-Style Beef Pops

27 minutes

Yield: 4 servings

Reminiscent of authentic Moroccan kefta, these hand-held kabobs make for a fun family dinner.

½ cup (125 mL) fresh mint leaves, divided

1 slice white sandwich bread

2 shallots

2 garlic cloves, peeled

⅓ cup (75 mL) plain nonfat Greek yogurt

1 tbsp (15 mL) ground cumin

1 tbsp (15 mL) water

¾ tsp (4 mL) ground black pepper

1 tsp (5 mL) salt, divided

1 lb (450 g) 80% lean ground beef

8 (8-10-in./20-25-cm) bamboo skewers

½ seedless cucumber

6 radishes

1 tbsp (15 mL) white wine vinegar

Crumbled feta cheese (optional)

1. Set aside six mint leaves. Tear bread into pieces. Place bread pieces, remaining mint, shallots and garlic into **Manual Food Processor**; process until finely chopped.

2. In large **Bamboo Fiber Bowl**, combine mint mixture, yogurt, cumin, water, pepper and *¾ tsp (4 mL)* of the salt; mix well. Add beef; mix gently but thoroughly until yogurt mixture is incorporated into beef.

3. Using a rounded **Large Scoop**, place eight scoops of beef mixture onto **Flexible Cutting Mat**. Roll each scoop into a 4-in. (10-cm) cylinder; thread onto skewers.

4. Place skewers on **Double Burner Griddle**. Cook over medium heat 9-11 minutes or until browned on all sides, turning occasionally (see Cook's Tip).

5. Meanwhile for salad, thinly slice cucumber and radishes using **Simple Slicer** on #2 setting. Cut slices in half.

6. Thinly slice reserved mint leaves using **Color Coated Nakiri Knife**.

7. Combine cucumber, radishes, reserved mint, vinegar and remaining ¼ tsp (1 mL) salt in **Small Batter Bowl**; mix well. Sprinkle salad with feta, if desired. Serve with beef pops.

Cook's Tips:

To get uniformly round pops, after threading the meat onto skewers, roll them on the cutting mat until all the edges are rounded.

The cooked sides of the beef pops will flatten slightly. This will allow you to lean the beef pops on one another as they cook so they will cook evenly.

U.S. Nutrients per serving (2 beef pops and ¾ cup/175 mL salad): **Calories** 340, **Total Fat** 23 g, **Saturated Fat** 9 g, **Cholesterol** 80 mg, **Sodium** 700 mg, **Carbohydrate** 9 g, **Fiber** 2 g, **Protein** 23 g

U.S. Diabetic exchanges per serving: ½ Starch, 3 Med-Fat Meat, 1½ Fat (½ Carb)

Smoky Black-Eyed Pea Soup

28 minutes

Get slow-cooked flavor fast with this hearty soup.

Yield: 8 servings
(12 cups/2.8 L)

1   slice (8 oz/250 g) smoked deli ham

1   large onion

2   tsp (10 mL) canola oil

1   medium sweet potato (about 12 oz/350 g)

2   tsp (10 mL) smoked paprika

6   cups (1.5 L) chicken stock, divided

⅓   cup (75 mL) flour

6   sprigs fresh thyme

2   cans (15.5 oz or 439 mL each) black-eyed peas, drained and rinsed

½   tsp (2 mL) *each* salt and ground black pepper

1   can (14.5 oz or 398 mL) stewed tomatoes

1   bunch collard greens (about 6 cups/1.5 L coarsely chopped)

1. Dice ham into ½-in. (1-cm) pieces using **Santoku Knife**.

2. Chop onion using **Food Chopper**. Add ham, onion and oil to **(4.75-qt./4.5-L) Casserole**. Cook over medium-high heat 2-3 minutes or until onion is softened, stirring occasionally.

3. Meanwhile, peel and dice sweet potato into ½-in. (1-cm) pieces. Add sweet potato and paprika to Casserole. Cook 30-60 seconds or until very fragrant, stirring occasionally.

4. Combine *1 cup (250 mL)* of the stock and flour in **Small Batter Bowl**; whisk well and set aside.

5. Place thyme into **Herb Infuser**. Add Herb Infuser, remaining 5 cups (1.25 L) stock, peas, salt and pepper to Casserole.

6. Place tomatoes into small **Bamboo Fiber Bowl**. Coarsely chop tomatoes using **Salad Chopper**; add to Casserole.

7. Cover and bring soup to a simmer. Whisk in flour mixture; cook 4-5 minutes or until sweet potatoes are tender.

8. Coarsely chop collard greens (see Cook's Tip); stir into soup. Return to a simmer. Remove Herb Infuser using **Chef's Tongs**. Serve soup.

Cook's Tips:

If desired, 1 tsp (5 mL) dried thyme leaves can be substituted for the fresh thyme. Add dried thyme in Step 3 with the sweet potato and paprika.

To coarsely chop collard greens, cut along the stem to remove leafy green parts. Discard stems. Stack leaves; cut lengthwise into strips, then cut crosswise.

U.S. Nutrients per serving (1½ cups/375 mL): **Calories** 190, **Total Fat** 2.5 g, **Saturated Fat** 0 g, **Cholesterol** 15 mg, **Sodium** 1150 mg, **Carbohydrate** 29 g, **Fiber** 5 g, **Protein** 14 g

U.S. Diabetic exchanges per serving: 1½ Starch, 1 Vegetable, 1 Lean Meat (1½ Carb)

Tangy Steaks with Shaved Vegetables

You won't miss the potatoes with this light, summery steak presentation.

⅔ cup (150 mL) white balsamic vinegar, divided

2½ tbsp (37 mL) **Rosemary-Infused Canola Oil**, divided

4 garlic cloves, pressed

1 tsp (5 mL) salt, divided

¾ tsp (4 mL) ground black pepper, divided

2 New York strip steaks, cut ¾ in. (2 cm) thick (8 oz/250 g each)

1 large carrot

½ medium zucchini

1 small fennel bulb, trimmed

2 tsp (10 mL) sugar

Grilled Ciabatta (optional)

1. For marinade, whisk together *½ cup (125 mL)* of the vinegar, *2 tbsp (30 mL)* of the oil, pressed garlic and *½ tsp (2 mL) each* of the salt and pepper in **Small Batter Bowl**.

2. Prick steaks several times with **Hold 'N Slice®**. Cut steaks in half crosswise. Place steaks in large resealable plastic bag; add marinade and turn to coat. Refrigerate 10 minutes.

3. Meanwhile, cut carrot and zucchini into long ribbons using **Vegetable Peeler**, avoiding seeds of zucchini. Core and thinly slice fennel using **Simple Slicer** on #1 setting. Combine carrot, zucchini and fennel in large **Bamboo Fiber Bowl**.

4. For dressing, mix remaining 2½ tbsp (37 mL) vinegar, ½ tbsp (7 mL) oil, ½ tsp (2 mL) salt and ¼ tsp (1 mL) pepper and sugar in **Small Batter Bowl**. Pour dressing over vegetables; toss to coat.

5. If preparing *Grilled Ciabatta*, heat **Grill Pan** over medium-high heat 5 minutes. Split two square 4 oz (125 g) ciabatta rolls in half to make four squares. Brush bread with an additional 1½ tbsp (22 mL) Rosemary-Infused Canola Oil. Place bread into pan; top with **Grill Press** and grill 45-60 seconds per side or until grill marks appear. Remove bread from pan.

6. Remove steaks from marinade *(do not discard marinade)*. Lightly spray pan with olive oil using **Kitchen Spritzer**. Cook steaks 2-3 minutes per side or until **Pocket Thermometer** registers 145°F (63°C) for medium-rare doneness.

7. For sauce, pour marinade into **(1.5-qt./1.4-L) Saucepan**. Bring to a boil over medium heat; cook 1 minute.

8. Serve steaks with sauce, vegetables and *Grilled Ciabatta*, if desired.

Cook's Tip:

If desired, 2 tbsp (30 mL) canola oil and 2 tsp (10 mL) finely chopped fresh rosemary leaves can be substituted for the Rosemary-Infused Canola Oil in the marinade. For the dressing, combine ½ tbsp (7 mL) canola oil with ½ tsp (2 mL) finely chopped fresh rosemary leaves.

U.S. Nutrients per serving: **Calories** 390, **Total Fat** 18 g, **Saturated Fat** 4 g, **Cholesterol** 90 mg, **Sodium** 690 mg, **Carbohydrate** 24 g, **Fiber** 3 g, **Protein** 34 g

U.S. Diabetic exchanges per serving: 5 Vegetable, 3 Med-Fat Meat, 1 Fat (0 Carb)

Saucy Chorizo & Egg Tostadas

28 minutes

Yield: 6 servings

This savory Mexican dish requires no fork or knife; pick them up and dig in!

½   medium onion

12   oz (350 g) pork chorizo sausage

1   cup (250 mL) enchilada sauce, divided

6   eggs

½   cup (125 mL) shredded Chihuahua cheese

½   head iceberg lettuce (about 3 cups/750 mL thinly sliced)

2   vine-ripened tomatoes

1   avocado

¼   cup (50 mL) fresh cilantro

12   corn tostadas

1. Chop onion using **Food Chopper**. Add onion and chorizo to **(10-in./24-cm) Skillet** *(do not use stainless cookware)*. Cook over medium-high heat 8-10 minutes or until chorizo is cooked through, breaking into crumbles halfway through cooking using **Mix 'N Chop**.

2. Stir *half* of the enchilada sauce into the chorizo mixture; cook 1-2 minutes or until heated through. Transfer to **Classic Batter Bowl**; keep warm. Wipe Skillet clean.

3. Meanwhile, lightly beat eggs in **Small Batter Bowl**. Lightly spray Skillet with canola oil using **Kitchen Spritzer**.

4. Cook eggs over medium heat 4-6 minutes or until set but still moist, stirring occasionally. Sprinkle with cheese; cover. Remove Skillet from heat.

5. Thinly slice lettuce using **Chef's Knife**. Slice tomatoes; cut slices in half. Peel and slice avocado lengthwise and chop cilantro.

6. To serve, top tostadas with lettuce, chorizo mixture, eggs, cilantro, tomatoes and avocado. Drizzle with remaining enchilada sauce.

Cook's Tips:

Different brands of chorizo will yield varying amounts of fat. Drain the fat from the chorizo after cooking, if necessary. For best results, purchase chorizo from the meat counter if available.

Green or red enchilada sauce can be used in this recipe.

To clean the Skillet in Step 2, grab two folded paper towels with tongs and wipe the Skillet clean.

U.S. Nutrients per serving (2 tostadas): **Calories** 550, **Total Fat** 40 g, **Saturated Fat** 13 g, **Cholesterol** 245 mg, **Sodium** 1130 mg, **Carbohydrate** 24 g, **Fiber** 4 g, **Protein** 25 g

U.S. Diabetic exchanges per serving: 1½ Starch, 3 High-Fat Meat, 3 Fat (1½ Carb)

Maple Herb & Bacon Wrapped Pork

Yield: 4 servings

How do you make pork even tastier? Wrap it in bacon and served with a tangy slaw!

1 pork tenderloin (about 1¼ lbs/575 g)

2 tbsp (30 mL) **Maple Herb Rub**

6 slices uncooked bacon

¼ small head red cabbage (about 1½ cups/375 mL thinly sliced)

½ cup (125 mL) water

2 tbsp (30 mL) brown sugar

1½ tbsp (22 mL) cider vinegar

¼ tsp (1 mL) salt

⅛ tsp (0.5 mL) ground black pepper

1 medium carrot

1 medium red apple such as Jonathan or Fuji

1. Preheat oven to 450°F (230°C). Trim fat and silver skin from pork. Coat pork evenly with rub.

2. Wrap pork with bacon, slightly overlapping slices by about ¼ in. (6 mm). Secure bacon with wooden picks. Cook pork in **11-** or **12-in. (28-** or **30-cm) Skillet** over medium-high heat 5-6 minutes or until browned on all sides, turning occasionally.

3. Transfer pork to **Large Sheet Pan**. Bake 14-16 minutes or until **Pocket Thermometer** registers 145°F (63°C). Drain all but 1 tbsp (15 mL) of the bacon drippings from Skillet.

4. For slaw, thinly slice cabbage using **Santoku Knife**. Add cabbage, water, brown sugar, vinegar, salt and pepper to Skillet. Cook, covered, over medium-low heat 8-10 minutes or until cabbage is wilted, stirring occasionally.

5. Meanwhile, cut carrot into julienne strips using **Julienne Peeler**. Thinly slice apple. Add carrot and apple to Skillet; cook 3-4 minutes or until crisp-tender.

6. Remove pork from oven to **Large Grooved Cutting Board**. Remove wooden picks. Slice pork into medallions; serve with slaw.

Cook's Tips:

When securing the pork with wooden picks, be sure to thread them through the bacon slices several times to ensure that the bacon doesn't fall off during cooking.

When roasting the pork in the oven, be aware of the thickness of the tenderloin. A thicker tenderloin will roast at the higher end of the time frame while a thinner tenderloin will roast at the lower end.

U.S. Nutrients per serving: **Calories** 320, **Total Fat** 12 g, **Saturated Fat** 4 g, **Cholesterol** 110 mg, **Sodium** 660 mg, **Carbohydrate** 17 g, **Fiber** 2 g, **Protein** 35 g

U.S. Diabetic exchanges per serving: 1 Fruit, 5 Lean Meat (1 Carb)

Ginger Citrus Steak Salad

26 minutes

Yield: 6 servings

This salad pops with its combination of tangy Asian dressing, tender steak and crunchy chow mein noodles.

1   lb (450 g) skirt steak
⅓   cup (75 mL) rice vinegar
⅓   cup (75 mL) soy sauce
3½   tbsp (52 mL) brown sugar
2½   tbsp (37 mL)
     Ginger Citrus Rub
3   garlic cloves, pressed
1   tbsp (15 mL) canola oil
½   tsp (2 mL) toasted sesame oil
1   large head napa cabbage
     (about 8 cups/2 L
     thinly sliced)
2   medium carrots
2   cups (500 mL) chow
     mein noodles
1   cup (250 mL) frozen shelled
     edamame beans, thawed
5   oz (150 g) sliced
     shiitake mushrooms

1. Pound steak using toothed side of **Meat Tenderizer**. Cut steak into thin slices using **Santoku Knife** (see Cook's Tip). Place in **Classic Batter Bowl**.

2. Combine vinegar, soy sauce, brown sugar, rub and garlic pressed with **Garlic Press** in **Small Batter Bowl**. Pour ¼ cup (50 mL) of the vinegar mixture over steak and mix well.

3. For dressing, whisk oils into remaining vinegar mixture in Small Batter Bowl. Set aside.

4. Lightly spray **11-** or **12-in. (28-** or **30-cm) Skillet** with canola oil using **Kitchen Spritzer**. Heat over medium-high heat 1-3 minutes or until shimmering. Remove steak from marinade; discard marinade. Add steak to Skillet; cook undisturbed 2-4 minutes or until browned.

5. As steak cooks, thinly slice cabbage. Cut carrots into julienne strips using **Julienne Peeler**. Place cabbage, carrots, noodles and edamame in **Large Bamboo Round Bowl**.

6. Add mushrooms to Skillet; cook 2-3 minutes or until mushrooms are cooked, stirring occasionally.

7. Remove Skillet from heat. Add steak mixture and dressing to cabbage mixture; mix well and serve.

Cook's Tips:

Skirt steak should always be sliced against the grain, or it can be tough. The grain of the meat is the direction the fibers of the muscle run. By cutting the strip of meat into short sections, you can easily slice against the grain for the most tender results.

If desired, 1 tbsp (15 mL) fresh orange juice, ½ tbsp (7 mL) fresh lime juice, 2 tsp (10 mL) grated fresh gingerroot, 2 pressed garlic cloves and ½ tsp (2 mL) salt can be substituted for the Ginger Citrus Rub.

U.S. Nutrients per serving: **Calories** 360, **Total Fat** 19 g, **Saturated Fat** 5 g, **Cholesterol** 45 mg, **Sodium** 890 mg, **Carbohydrate** 24 g, **Fiber** 5 g, **Protein** 23 g

U.S. Diabetic exchanges per serving: 1½ Starch, 3 Med-Fat Meat (1½ Carb)

Gravy-Smothered Sausage Burgers

These over-the-top burgers are topped with a simple gravy that is made right in the microwave!

Yield: 4 servings

Burgers
1   large tomato
1   small yellow onion
5   slices Texas toast, divided
1   egg
1   lb (450 g) bulk pork sausage
2   cups (500 mL) baby spinach leaves

Gravy
1½   tbsp (22 mL) flour
1   tbsp (15 mL) butter, melted
½   cup (125 mL) chicken stock
⅓   cup (75 mL) milk
1   garlic clove, pressed
⅛   tsp (0.5 mL) ground black pepper
1   tbsp (15 mL) snipped fresh chives

1. Slice tomato into four slices; set aside. Finely chop onion using **Food Chopper**.

2. Remove and discard crusts from one slice of Texas toast; tear bread into pieces. Combine bread pieces, onion and egg in **Stainless (4-qt./4-L) Mixing Bowl**; mix until a smooth paste forms.

3. Add sausage to mixing bowl; mix gently but thoroughly. Form sausage mixture into four ½-inch-thick (1-cm) patties.

4. Heat **Grill Pan** over medium heat 2 minutes. Spray remaining bread slices with canola oil using **Kitchen Spritzer**. Grill bread 1-2 minutes per side or until grill marks appear; remove bread from pan.

5. Add patties to pan; grill 4-6 minutes per side or until internal temperature reaches 165°F (74°C).

6. Meanwhile, to make gravy, whisk together flour and butter in **Small Batter Bowl**. Whisk in stock, milk, pressed garlic and pepper. Microwave, uncovered, on HIGH 1-3 minutes or until thick, whisking halfway through. Remove batter bowl from microwave; whisk gravy until smooth.

7. To assemble burgers, top grilled toasts with spinach, tomato and burgers; drizzle with gravy and sprinkle with chives.

Cook's Tips:

Bulk pork sausage does not have a casing and usually comes in a tubular package. It can be found in the refrigerated section near the bacon and breakfast sausage links.

The key to making a smooth gravy (without lumps) is to whisk the flour and butter together until the flour completely dissolves, then add the liquid.

U.S. Nutrients per serving: **Calories** 600, **Total Fat** 37 g, **Saturated Fat** 14 g, **Cholesterol** 135 mg, **Sodium** 1180 mg, **Carbohydrate** 40 g, **Fiber** 3 g, **Protein** 26 g

U.S. Diabetic exchanges per serving: 2½ Starch, 1 Vegetable, 2½ High-Fat Meat, 3 Fat (2½ Carb)

Porcini Beef Filets with Red Wine Syrup

28 minutes

Yield: 4 servings

A savory mushroom crust surrounds tender beef filets in this simple, yet sophisticated recipe.

3   shallots

2   cups (500 mL) dry red wine such as Cabernet Sauvignon

½   cup (125 mL) sugar

8   stems fresh thyme plus 2 tsp (10 mL) leaves, divided

1   tsp (5 mL) ground black pepper, divided

1   pkg (½ oz/15 g) dried porcini mushrooms

4   beef tenderloin filets (4 oz/125 g each)

3   tbsp (45 mL) olive oil, divided

½   tsp (2 mL) salt

8   oz (250 g) fresh green beans, trimmed

1. Preheat oven to 400°F (200°C). For syrup, finely chop shallots using **Food Chopper**. Combine shallots, wine, sugar, thyme stems and *½ tsp (2 mL)* of the pepper in **(3-qt./2.8-L) Saucepan**. Bring to a rapid boil over high heat. Cook 13-15 minutes or until thick and syrupy.

2. Meanwhile, combine mushrooms and 2 tsp (10 mL) of the thyme leaves in **Manual Food Processor**; process until finely chopped.

3. Brush filets with *1 tbsp (15 mL)* of the oil. Season with salt and remaining ½ tsp (2 mL) pepper. Generously coat filets on all sides with mushroom mixture (see Cook's Tip).

4. Heat remaining oil in **(10-in./24-cm) Skillet** over medium heat 1-3 minutes or until shimmering. Add filets, cook 2-3 minutes or until browned. Turn filets over and place Skillet into oven.

5. Bake 3-4 minutes or until **Pocket Thermometer** registers 140°F (60°F) for medium-rare doneness.

6. Place **(5-in./13-cm) Strainer** over **(1-cup/250-mL) Prep Bowl**. Strain syrup into prep bowl; discard shallots and thyme stems.

7. Add green beans and enough water to cover in **Large Micro-Cooker®**. Microwave, covered, on HIGH 2-3 minutes or until crisp-tender. Serve filets with syrup and green beans.

Cook's Tips:

For best results, ask your butcher for center-cut filets to ensure they cook evenly.

To generously coat the filets, place them on a **Flexible Cutting Mat**. Brush with oil and season as directed; then roll the filets in the mushroom mixture to coat evenly.

U.S. Nutrients per serving: **Calories** 600, **Total Fat** 31 g, **Saturated Fat** 10 g, **Cholesterol** 95 mg, **Sodium** 360 mg, **Carbohydrate** 34 g, **Fiber** 2 g, **Protein** 25 g

U.S. Diabetic exchanges per serving: 2 Fruit, 1 Vegetable, 3 Med-Fat Meat, 3 Fat (2 Carb)

Stuffed Hash Brown Omelet p. 113

Hearty Mushroom Goulash p. 115

Mushroom-Stuffed Tofu p. 121

Couscous Cakes with Cucumber Salad p. 125

meatless
DISHES

Try something new for dinner with vegetarian entrées that are sure to impress.

Linguine with Creamy Asparagus Pesto

Pasta and a homemade pesto ready to eat in 25 minutes – that's impressive!

Yield: 6 servings

Pasta

1   tsp (5 mL) salt (optional)

12   oz (350 g) uncooked linguine pasta

Pesto

1   lb (450 g) fresh asparagus spears, trimmed (see Cook's Tip)

⅓   cup (75 mL) snipped fresh chives

2   oz (60 g) fresh Parmesan cheese

1   lemon

¼   cup (50 mL) dry-roasted salted pistachios, shelled

¼   cup (50 mL) canola oil

1   garlic clove, peeled

1   medium avocado

¾   tsp (4 mL) *each* salt and ground black pepper

¼   tsp (1 mL) sugar

Additional ground black pepper (optional)

1. For pasta, bring 3 qt. (3 L) water and salt, if desired, to a boil in covered **(4-qt./3.8-L) Casserole**. Cook pasta according to package directions; drain using medium **Stainless Mesh Colander**.

2. Meanwhile, to prepare pesto, place asparagus and enough water to cover in **Large Micro-Cooker®**. Microwave, covered, on HIGH 7-9 minutes (see Cook's Tip) or until tender; drain and cool 5 minutes.

3. Snip chives; set aside. Grate cheese with **Rotary Grater**. Juice lemon to measure 1 tbsp (15 mL).

4. Slice tips off asparagus spears; set tips aside. Slice asparagus bottoms into 1-in. (2.5-cm) pieces. Process asparagus bottoms, lemon juice, pistachios, oil and garlic in **Manual Food Processor** until finely chopped. Add half of the cheese, avocado, salt, pepper and sugar; process until smooth.

5. Using **Chef's Tongs**, toss pasta, pesto, chives and asparagus tips in **Stainless (4-qt./4-L) Mixing Bowl** until pasta is thoroughly coated.

6. Sprinkle pasta with remaining cheese and additional pepper, if desired.

Cook's Tips:

To trim asparagus, snap off the bottoms of the spears. The tough stringy ends easily break from the more tender part of the asparagus.

The thickness of asparagus spears can vary greatly. If using very thin spears, start with around 5 minutes in the microwave, then increase as needed to cook through. If using thicker spears, start at the low end of the recommended time and continue cooking as needed.

U.S. Nutrients per serving: **Calories** 420, **Total Fat** 20 g, **Saturated Fat** 3.5 g, **Cholesterol** 5 mg, **Sodium** 450 mg, **Carbohydrate** 50 g, **Fiber** 6 g, **Protein** 14 g

U.S. Diabetic exchanges per serving: 2½ Starch, 2½ Vegetable, 3½ Fat (2½ Carb)

Simmered Eggs in Spicy Tomato Sauce

Yield: 4 servings

This version of eggs in purgatory boasts a spicy sauce made with fresh tomatoes!

1	medium poblano pepper
1	jalapeño pepper
1	medium yellow onion
3	garlic cloves, peeled
2	tsp (10 mL) ground cumin
4	medium vine-ripened tomatoes
1	tbsp (15 mL) olive oil
1	can (8 oz or 213 mL) tomato sauce
¾	tsp (4 mL) salt
½	tsp (2 mL) sugar
8	eggs
4	oz (125 g) queso fresco cheese (see Cook's Tip)
½	cup (125 mL) fresh cilantro
4	corn tostadas

1. Remove seeds from peppers. Cut peppers and onion into chunks.

2. Process peppers, onion, garlic and cumin in **Manual Food Processor** until coarsely chopped. Transfer mixture to **Small Batter Bowl**.

3. Cut tomatoes into quarters. Process half of the tomatoes in processor until coarsely chopped; pour into **Classic Batter Bowl**. Repeat with remaining tomatoes.

4. Heat oil in **11-** or **12-in. (28-** or **30-cm) Skillet** over medium heat 1-3 minutes or until shimmering. Cook pepper mixture 2-3 minutes or until crisp-tender.

5. Stir in chopped tomatoes, tomato sauce, salt and sugar. Cook, covered, 3-4 minutes or until mixture comes to a boil; reduce heat to a simmer.

6. Crack one egg into **(1-cup/250-mL) Prep Bowl** and gently add to tomato sauce in Skillet. Repeat with remaining eggs, spacing 1-in. (2.5-cm) apart. Cook eggs 6-8 minutes or according to desired doneness.

7. Crumble cheese with **Easy Release Cheese Crumbler**. Coarsely chop cilantro.

8. Divide tomato sauce and eggs among serving bowls; sprinkle with cheese and cilantro. Serve with tostadas.

Cook's Tips:

Queso fresco can be found in the specialty cheese section of most grocery stores. If desired, feta cheese can be substituted for the queso fresco.

To make this recipe even spicier, leave the seeds in the jalapeño pepper.

U.S. Nutrients per serving: **Calories** 320, **Total Fat** 18 g, **Saturated Fat** 5 g, **Cholesterol** 375 mg, **Sodium** 950 mg, **Carbohydrate** 23 g, **Fiber** 4 g, **Protein** 18 g

U.S. Diabetic exchanges per serving: 1 Starch, 1½ Vegetable, 2 Med-Fat Meat, 1 Fat (1 Carb)

Tofu Tikka Masala

25 minutes

Yield: 4 servings

Authentic Indian flavors shine in this "tastes like it took all day" tofu dish.

1 cup (250 mL) uncooked basmati rice

¼ cup (50 mL) fresh cilantro

1 jalapeño pepper

1 medium onion

2 tbsp (30 mL) vegetable oil

2 tbsp (30 mL) mild Indian curry paste (see Cook's Tip)

1 can (13.5 oz/398 mL) lite coconut milk

1 can (8 oz or 213 mL) tomato sauce

1 tbsp (15 mL) brown sugar

½ tsp (2 mL) salt

1 tbsp (15 mL) cornstarch dissolved in 1 tbsp (15 mL) cold water

1 pkg (14 oz or 397 g) extra-firm tofu, drained and patted dry

2 cups (500 mL) baby spinach leaves

¼ cup (50 mL) plain Greek yogurt (optional)

1. Rinse rice under warm running water 1 minute in **(7-in./18-cm) Strainer**, gently shaking to remove excess starch.

2. Combine rice and 2 cups (500 mL) water in **Rice Cooker Plus**. Microwave, covered, on HIGH 10 minutes. Let stand, covered, 10 minutes.

3. Meanwhile, chop cilantro using **Food Chopper** and set aside. Remove seeds from jalapeño. Chop jalapeño and onion.

4. Add onion, jalapeño, oil and curry paste to **(4-qt./3.8-L) Casserole**; cook over medium heat 6-8 minutes or until vegetables are tender, stirring occasionally.

5. Stir in coconut milk, tomato sauce, brown sugar and salt. Cover and bring to a simmer. Reduce heat to medium-low and slowly add cornstarch mixture, whisking constantly. Cook an additional 2-3 minutes or until thickened.

6. Meanwhile, dice tofu into 1-in. (2.5-cm) pieces. Gently stir in tofu, spinach and cilantro. Cook 5 minutes or until heated through and spinach is wilted. Serve stew over rice; top with yogurt, if desired.

Cook's Tips:

Indian curry paste can be found in the ethnic section of the grocery store. It comes in a jar which can be opened and then refrigerated for later use. Feel free to use a spicier paste in this recipe for additional kick!

For a less spicy version of this recipe, omit the jalapeño pepper.

U.S. Nutrients per serving: **Calories** 450, **Total Fat** 20 g, **Saturated Fat** 6 g, **Cholesterol** 0 mg, **Sodium** 780 mg, **Carbohydrate** 55 g, **Fiber** 5 g, **Protein** 15 g

U.S. Diabetic exchanges per serving: 3 Starch, 2 Vegetable, 4 Fat (3 Carb)

Creamy Cauliflower Soup

28 minutes

Yield: 6 servings
(about 7 cups/1.8 L)

Warm up with a simple main dish soup accentuated with garlic and herb-flavored cheese spread.

6   cups (1.5 L) cauliflower florets (about 1 small head)

3   cups (750 mL) water

½   loaf (8 oz/250 g) whole grain baguette

2   medium onions

5   garlic cloves, peeled and divided

1   tbsp (15 mL) olive oil

½   cup (125 mL) fresh basil leaves

2   oz (60 g) fresh Parmesan cheese

1   container (6.5 oz or 150 g) garlic and herb flavored cheese spread such as *Boursin*®

1   tsp (5 mL) salt

1. Preheat oven to 400°F (200°C). Place cauliflower into large **Bamboo Fiber Bowl**. Chop into very small pieces using **Salad Chopper**. Add cauliflower and water to **Large Micro-Cooker®**. Microwave, covered, on HIGH 14-16 minutes or until cauliflower is very tender *(do not drain)*.

2. Meanwhile, slice baguette on a bias into eighteen ¼-in. (6-mm) slices. Arrange slices on **Cookie Sheet** and spray with olive oil using **Kitchen Spritzer**. Bake 9-11 minutes or until crisp.

3. Thinly slice onions using **Chef's Knife**. Combine onions, *4 of the garlic cloves* pressed with **Garlic Press** and oil in **(4.75-qt./4.5-L) Casserole**. Cook over medium heat 5-6 minutes or until onions are softened.

4. Cut remaining garlic clove in half. While holding bread with **Chef's Tongs**, rub cut side of garlic on surface of each bread slice.

5. Coarsely chop basil. Grate Parmesan using **Rotary Grater**.

6. Carefully ladle half of the cauliflower mixture and half of the onion mixture into blender container; cover and blend until smooth (see Cook's Tip). Pour blended soup into **Stainless (4-qt./4-L) Mixing Bowl**. Repeat with remaining cauliflower and onion mixtures.

7. Return soup to Casserole; bring to a simmer over medium-high heat. Whisk in cheeses and salt. Ladle soup into serving bowls. Garnish soup with basil and serve with bread.

Cook's Tips:

As the blender is running and the soup appears to be puréed, blend it another 30 seconds. This additional blending time will ensure a velvety texture.

If desired, repeat Steps 2 and 4 with the remaining baguette half and reserve these crispy, garlic-flavored toast points for another use.

U.S. Nutrients per serving (about 1¼ cups/300 mL soup, 3 bread slices): **Calories** 340, **Total Fat** 21 g, **Saturated Fat** 12 g, **Cholesterol** 40 mg, **Sodium** 920 mg, **Carbohydrate** 27 g, **Fiber** 6 g, **Protein** 13 g

U.S. Diabetic exchanges per serving: 1½ Starch, 1 Vegetable, 1 High-Fat Meat, 2 Fat (1½ Carb)

Stuffed Hash Brown Omelet

A crispy hash brown is folded over veggies and cheese to make an exceptional omelet.

Yield: 4 servings

½ small onion

½ small zucchini

2 garlic cloves, peeled

½ small red bell pepper

3 tbsp (45 mL) canola oil, divided

2 egg whites

3½ cups (875 mL) frozen shredded hash brown potatoes, thawed

½ tsp (2 mL) *each* salt and ground black pepper, divided

1 jar (6.5 oz or 170 mL) marinated artichokes, drained

½ cup (125 mL) fresh basil leaves

4 oz (125 g) shredded Italian cheese blend, divided

1. Coarsely chop onion, zucchini and garlic using **Food Chopper**. Dice bell pepper using **Santoku Knife**.

2. Heat *1 tbsp (15 mL)* of the oil in **(11-in./28-cm) Skillet** (see Cook's Tip) over medium-high heat 1-3 minutes or until shimmering. Place onion, zucchini, garlic and bell pepper into Skillet; cook 3-4 minutes or until crisp-tender, stirring occasionally. Transfer vegetables to **Small Batter Bowl**.

3. Meanwhile, whisk egg whites in **Classic Batter Bowl** until frothy. Add potatoes and ¼ tsp (1 mL) *each* of the salt and black pepper; mix well.

4. Add remaining *2 tbsp (30 mL)* oil to Skillet; heat over medium-high heat 1-2 minutes or until shimmering. Add potato mixture; using **Slotted Turner**, press potatoes down firmly into Skillet. Cook, covered, 7-8 minutes or until golden brown on bottom.

5. Meanwhile, chop artichokes using **Food Chopper**. Chop basil. Add artichokes, basil, *half* of the cheese and remaining ¼ tsp (1 mL) *each* salt and black pepper to vegetables.

6. Sprinkle remaining cheese over potatoes. Top half of the potatoes with vegetable mixture; fold in half omelet-style. Remove Skillet from heat; cover and let stand 3 minutes. Cut into 4 wedges and serve.

Cook's Tip:

To make this recipe in a **(12-in./30-cm) Skillet**, press potato mixture to within 1-in. (2.5-cm) from sides of Skillet. Continue as recipe directs. *(Do not use stainless cookware to prepare this recipe or the potatoes will stick to the Skillet.)*

U.S. Nutrients per serving: **Calories** 340, **Total Fat** 28 g, **Saturated Fat** 12 g, **Cholesterol** 35 mg, **Sodium** 830 mg, **Carbohydrate** 33 g, **Fiber** 4 g, **Protein** 12 g

U.S. Diabetic exchanges per serving: 2 Starch, ½ Vegetable, 1 Med-Fat Meat, 4 Fat (2 Carb)

Hearty Mushroom Goulash

You won't miss the meat in this savory vegetarian version of a mealtime classic!

½ pkg (14.5 oz or 411 g) uncooked multi grain farfalle pasta (3 cups/750 mL)

2 tbsp (30 mL) olive oil

1 medium onion

1 lb (450 g) sliced cremini mushrooms

1½ cups (375 mL) vegetable broth

½ cup (125 mL) dry white wine such as Chardonnay or Sauvignon Blanc

¼ cup (50 mL) tomato paste

2 tbsp (30 mL) flour

2 tsp (10 mL) smoked paprika

3 garlic cloves, pressed

¾ tsp (4 mL) salt

½ tsp (2 mL) ground black pepper

¼ cup (50 mL) fresh parsley

1 cup (250 mL) frozen peas, thawed

½ cup (125 mL) sour cream

1. Cook pasta according to package directions, omitting salt and oil.

2. Heat oil in **11-** or **12-in. (28-** or **30-cm) Skillet** over medium-high heat 1-3 minutes or until shimmering. Finely chop onion using **Food Chopper**.

3. Add mushrooms to Skillet; cook 4-6 minutes or until browned. Add onion; cook an additional 2-3 minutes or until onion is softened, stirring occasionally.

4. Meanwhile, combine broth, wine, tomato paste and flour in **Small Batter Bowl**. Whisk well.

5. Add paprika and garlic pressed with **Garlic Press** to Skillet. Cook and stir 20-30 seconds or until fragrant.

6. Add broth mixture, salt and pepper to Skillet. Bring to a simmer. Reduce heat to medium and cook 3-4 minutes or until thickened, stirring occasionally.

7. Meanwhile, chop parsley using **Chef's Knife**. Remove Skillet from heat. Stir in peas and sour cream until incorporated.

8. Divide pasta into serving bowls and serve with goulash. Sprinkle with parsley.

Cook's Tips:

Cremini (sometimes spelled crimini) mushrooms are baby portobello mushrooms and can be found sliced or whole. They have a darker color and deeper mushroom flavor than domestic white mushrooms.

If desired, regular paprika can be substituted for the smoked paprika.

U.S. Nutrients per serving (1 cup/250 mL goulash, 1½ cups/375 mL pasta): **Calories** 420, **Total Fat** 14 g, **Saturated Fat** 4 g, **Cholesterol** 10 mg, **Sodium** 1010 mg, **Carbohydrate** 57 g, **Fiber** 8 g, **Protein** 16 g

U.S. Diabetic exchanges per serving: 3 Starch, 3 Vegetable, 2 Fat (3 Carb)

Warm Goat Cheese Salad with Apricot Dressing

Yield: 4 servings

Red quinoa gives a distinct nutty flavor to rich goat cheese and apricot dressing.

½ cup (125 mL) uncooked red quinoa, rinsed (see Cook's Tip)

⅛ tsp (0.5 mL) plus ¼ tsp (1 mL) salt, divided

¼ cup (50 mL) sliced almonds

¼ cup (50 mL) plain dry bread crumbs

¾ tsp (4 mL) dried thyme leaves, divided

2 pkgs (4 oz/125 g each) soft goat cheese

⅓ cup (75 mL) apricot preserves

3 tbsp (45 mL) oil

2 tbsp (30 mL) white wine vinegar

⅛ tsp (0.5 mL) ground black pepper

1 pkg (5 oz/150 g) mixed greens salad blend

1 pkg (6 oz/175 g) fresh raspberries

1. Bring 1 cup (250 mL) water to a boil in **(1.5-qt./1.4-L) Saucepan**. Add quinoa and *⅛ tsp (0.5 mL)* of the salt. Cover; reduce heat to low and simmer 15 minutes or until tender. Remove from heat.

2. Meanwhile, place almonds into **Small Micro-Cooker®**; cover and microwave on HIGH 1-2 minutes or until toasted, stirring every 30 seconds.

3. Mix bread crumbs and *½ tsp (2 mL)* of the thyme in **Coating Tray**. Slice cheese into eight slices; shape each slice into 2-in. (5-cm) rounds. Gently press cheese rounds into crumb mixture, coating on all sides.

4. For dressing, process apricot preserves, oil, vinegar, pepper and remaining ¼ tsp (1 mL) *each* salt and thyme in **Manual Food Processor** until blended. Stir 3 tbsp (45 mL) of the dressing into the quinoa.

5. Divide greens among four serving plates. Top evenly with quinoa, raspberries and almonds.

6. Spray **(10-in./24-cm) Sauté Pan** with canola oil using **Kitchen Spritzer**; heat over medium heat 1-3 minutes or until shimmering. Add cheese rounds; cook 25-30 seconds. Carefully turn cheese over using **Small Nylon Turner**; cook 25-30 seconds or until cheese is softened.

7. Place two cheese rounds on each salad; drizzle with remaining dressing.

Cook's Tips:

Rinsing quinoa before cooking helps remove the bitter taste.

This salad is great for an easy weeknight meal but elegant enough to serve guests. If desired, prepare the dressing and coat the goat cheese a day in advance. Refrigerate until ready to use.

U.S. Nutrients per serving: **Calories** 480, **Total Fat** 27 g, **Saturated Fat** 9 g, **Cholesterol** 25 mg, **Sodium** 500 mg, **Carbohydrate** 44 g, **Fiber** 6 g, **Protein** 17 g

U.S. Diabetic exchanges per serving: 1 Starch, 2 Fruit, 2 High-Fat Meat, 2 Fat (3 Carb)

Three Cheese 'N Apple Risotto

Yield: 4 servings

Parmesan, mascarpone and cheddar cheeses combine with apples for a knockout no-fuss dinner.

1 carton (32 oz or 900 mL) vegetable broth

2 tbsp (30 mL) slivered almonds

1 medium onion

2 tbsp (30 mL) olive oil

1⅓ cups (325 mL) uncooked Arborio rice

½ cup (125 mL) apple juice

½ tsp (2 mL) salt

2 small red apples such as Jonathan

1 oz (30 g) fresh Parmesan cheese

2 oz (60 g) mascarpone cheese

½ cup (125 mL) shredded sharp cheddar cheese

1. Heat broth in **(2-qt./1.9-L) Saucepan** over medium-high heat until simmering. Reduce heat to medium-low.

2. Meanwhile, place almonds in **Small Micro-Cooker®**. Microwave, covered, on HIGH 1-2 minutes or until light brown, stirring after 30 seconds. Set aside.

3. Chop onion using **Food Chopper**. Add onion, oil and rice to **11-** or **12-in. (28-** or **30-cm) Skillet**; cook over medium-high heat 2-3 minutes or until onion is softened and rice is translucent, stirring constantly with **Bamboo Spoon**.

4. Add apple juice and salt to Skillet; cook 1-2 minutes or until liquid is completely evaporated, stirring constantly.

5. Using **Ladle**, pour ½ cup (125 mL) of the hot broth into Skillet. Cook, uncovered, 2-3 minutes or until broth is absorbed, stirring constantly. Repeat with remaining broth in ½-cup (125-mL) increments, cooking and stirring 2-3 minutes after each addition until all of the broth has been added (about 18-20 minutes total cook time).

6. Dice apples using **Santoku Knife**. Grate Parmesan using **Rotary Grater**.

7. Reduce heat to low. Stir apples, Parmesan and mascarpone into rice mixture. Sprinkle with cheddar; cover and let stand 1 minute or until cheeses are melted. Top with almonds.

Cook's Tips:

Risotto's richness comes from the starchy Arborio rice. It's important to constantly stir as the risotto cooks to agitate the natural starches in the rice. The risotto mixture should constantly be simmering, absorbing the liquid as it cooks.

If desired, softened cream cheese can be substituted for the mascarpone.

U.S. Nutrients per serving: **Calories** 580, **Total Fat** 24 g, **Saturated Fat** 9 g, **Cholesterol** 40 mg, **Sodium** 1060 mg, **Carbohydrate** 79 g, **Fiber** 4 g, **Protein** 15 g

U.S. Diabetic exchanges per serving: 4 Starch, 1 Fruit, ½ High-Fat Meat, 3 Fat (5 Carb)

Mushroom-Stuffed Tofu

Take tofu to a whole new level with this fun idea for a meatless main dish.

Filling & Tofu

4	oz (125 g) cremini mushrooms
½	small onion
2	garlic cloves, peeled
3	tbsp (45 mL) canola oil, divided
2	tbsp (30 mL) reduced-sodium soy sauce
2	tbsp (30 mL) panko bread crumbs
1	pkg (14 oz or 397 g) extra-firm tofu, drained and patted dry
¼	cup (50 mL) cornstarch

Bok Choy & Sauce

4	heads baby bok choy
¼	cup (50 mL) reduced-sodium soy sauce
1	tbsp (15 mL) **Asian Seasoning Mix**
1	tbsp (15 mL) toasted sesame oil

1. For filling, process mushrooms in **Manual Food Processor** until finely chopped; remove mushrooms.

2. Add onion and garlic to processor; process until finely chopped.

3. Heat *1 tbsp (15 mL)* of the oil in **(10-in./24-cm) Sauté Pan** *(do not use stainless cookware)* over medium-high heat 1-3 minutes or until shimmering. Add mushrooms and onion mixture. Cook 5-6 minutes or until vegetables begin to brown, stirring occasionally.

4. Add soy sauce to pan. Cook an additional 1-2 minutes or until liquid is completely evaporated. Transfer filling to **Small Batter Bowl** and stir in panko crumbs.

5. As filling cooks, cut tofu in half lengthwise. Stand halves upright on **Cutting Board**. Create a lengthwise hole through the top of each half using **The Corer™** and remove centers. Place filling into a small resealable plastic bag. Trim ¾-in. (2-cm) from corner of the bag and pipe filling into centers of tofu (see Cook's Tip).

6. Slice bok choy in half lengthwise and remove cores. Place into **Large Micro-Cooker®** with ¼ cup (50 mL) water. Microwave, covered, on HIGH 2-3 minutes or until crisp-tender. Drain and set aside.

7. Heat remaining 2 tbsp (30 mL) oil in clean pan over medium-high heat 1-3 minutes or until shimmering. Place cornstarch into **Coating Tray**. Dredge all sides of tofu in cornstarch. Cook tofu 2-3 minutes per side or until browned on all sides.

8. Remove tofu from pan to cutting board. Cut each half into six slices using **Bread Knife**.

9. Whisk together soy sauce, seasoning mix and oil in **(1-cup/250-mL) Prep Bowl**. Serve tofu with sauce and bok choy.

Cook's Tips:

Don't discard the removed centers of the tofu! Dice and use for your next stir-fry or salad.

When filling the tofu, pack filling into tofu with your fingertip and add more filling. The tofu is properly filled when the sides begin to bulge slightly.

When slicing cooked tofu, begin slicing with little to no pressure, allowing the blade to penetrate the crust; then slice through with light pressure until you reach the bottom.

U.S. Nutrients per serving: **Calories** 290, **Total Fat** 19 g, **Saturated Fat** 1.5 g, **Cholesterol** 0 mg, **Sodium** 950 mg, **Carbohydrate** 18 g, **Fiber** 3 g, **Protein** 13 g

U.S. Diabetic exchanges per serving: ½ Starch, 2 Vegetable, 1 Lean Meat, 3 Fat (½ Carb)

Raspberry Habanero Monte Cristo Sandwiches

24 minutes

Yield: 4 servings

Give a classic sandwich an unexpected kick with sweet and spicy Raspberry Habanero Sauce.

1. Core apple using **The Corer™**. Slice apple using **Simple Slicer** on #2 setting.

2. Spread each bread slice with 1 tbsp (15 mL) of the sauce. Arrange 1 cheese slice and 3 apple slices over half of the bread slices. Top with an additional cheese slice and remaining bread slices, sauce side down.

3. Whisk together eggs, water and sage in **Coating Tray**.

4. Heat butter on **Double Burner Griddle** over medium heat 1 minute or until melted.

5. Dip sandwiches into egg mixture, coating all sides. Place onto Griddle. Cook 3-4 minutes per side or until golden brown and cheese is melted. Cut sandwiches in half. Sprinkle with powdered sugar, if desired.

1	Granny Smith apple
8	slices Italian bread (½ in./1 cm thick)
½	cup (125 mL) **Raspberry Habanero Sauce** (see Cook's Tip)
8	thin slices havarti cheese (6 oz/175 g)
3	eggs, beaten
6	tbsp (90 mL) water
½	tsp (2 mL) dried sage leaves
2	tbsp (30 mL) butter
	Powdered sugar (optional)

Cook's Tips:

If desired, ½ cup (125 mL) seedless raspberry jam mixed with ½ tsp (2 mL) cayenne pepper can be substituted for the Raspberry Habanero Sauce.

If desired, other "melting" cheeses such as Swiss or mozzarella cheese slices can be substituted for the havarti.

U.S. Nutrients per serving (1 sandwich): **Calories** 490, **Total Fat** 24 g, **Saturated Fat** 13 g, **Cholesterol** 185 mg, **Sodium** 710 mg, **Carbohydrate** 50 g, **Fiber** 3 g, **Protein** 21 g

U.S. Diabetic exchanges per serving: 2 Starch, 1½ Fruit, 2 High-Fat Meat, 1 Fat (3½ Carb)

Couscous Cakes
with Cucumber Salad

29 minutes

Yield: 4 servings

Flavors of the Mediterranean take center stage in these savory cakes.

1 cup (250 mL) uncooked plain couscous

3 tbsp (45 mL) olive oil, divided

2 tbsp (30 mL) **Bell Pepper Herb Rub**

½ seedless cucumber

⅓ cup (75 mL) fresh mint leaves

1½ cups (375 mL) grape tomatoes

⅓ cup (75 mL) pitted kalamata olives

¼ small red onion

1 lemon

4 oz (125 g) chive and onion cream cheese spread

4 oz (125 g) crumbled feta cheese, divided

1 egg

2 garlic cloves, pressed

Plain yogurt for serving (optional)

1. Prepare couscous according to package directions, omitting salt and adding *1 tbsp (15 mL)* of the oil and rub; set aside.

2. Meanwhile, for cucumber salad, dice cucumber and chop mint using **Santoku Knife**. Cut tomatoes and olives in half lengthwise. Chop onion using **Food Chopper**.

3. Juice lemon to measure 2 tbsp (30 mL). Combine juice, cucumber, mint, tomatoes, olives and onion in **Small Batter Bowl**; mix gently.

4. Combine couscous, cheese spread, *half* of the feta, egg and pressed garlic to **Classic Batter Bowl**; mix well.

5. Heat remaining 2 tbsp (30 mL) oil on **Square Griddle** over medium heat 1-3 minutes or until shimmering.

6. Form couscous mixture into 8 balls using rounded **Large Scoop**. Place couscous balls onto **Flexible Cutting Mat**; gently flatten into 2½-inch-wide (6-cm) patties. Add patties to Griddle; cook 2-3 minutes per side or until golden brown.

7. Serve cakes with cucumber salad; sprinkle salad with remaining feta. Serve with yogurt, if desired.

Cook's Tips:

These fun-to-make patties can be a little sticky! Wearing plastic gloves to prepare them will make it a little easier.

The cakes can be prepared several hours in advance. To prepare in advance, make the patties first and do not prepare the salad. After Step 6, cover cutting mat with plastic wrap and place in the refrigerator. When ready to serve, prepare the salad and cook the cakes as directed.

U.S. Nutrients per serving: **Calories** 470, **Total Fat** 27 g, **Saturated Fat** 11 g, **Cholesterol** 90 mg, **Sodium** 950 mg, **Carbohydrate** 42 g, **Fiber** 4 g, **Protein** 14 g

U.S. Diabetic exchanges per serving: 2½ Starch, 1 Vegetable, 1 Med-Fat Meat, 4 Fat (2½ Carb)

Recipe Index

ABOUT OUR RECIPES

All recipes were developed and carefully tested in The Pampered Chef® Test Kitchens. The recipes in this book have been designed to take you 29 minutes or less to prepare from start to finish, *including* preparation time needed for steps like chopping vegetables. The total time listed for each recipe includes all cooking, baking, cooling, chilling, standing and/or marinating time. In many cases, these steps are happening simultaneously. As an important first step, we suggest you read through the recipe and assemble the necessary ingredients and equipment. For best results, we recommend you use the ingredients indicated in the recipe.

NOTES ON NUTRITION

The nutrition information in *29 Minutes to Dinner, Volume 3* can help you decide how specific recipes can fit into your overall meal plan. The nutrient values for each recipe were derived from The Food Processor SQL Edition, Version 10.10.2 (ESHA Research), or are provided by food manufacturers. In addition to listing calories, total fat, saturated fat, cholesterol, sodium, carbohydrates, fiber and protein, we include two items commonly used by people with diabetes: diabetic food exchanges and carb choices. This information is based on the most current dietary guidelines, *Choose Your Foods: Exchange Lists for Diabetes Sixth Edition, 2008* by the American Diabetes Association® and the American Dietetic Association. Always consult with your physician, registered dietitian or certified diabetes educator who will address your individual needs.

Nutritional analysis for each recipe is based on the first serving yield whenever a range is given and the first ingredient listed whenever a choice is given and does not include optional ingredients, garnishes, fat used to grease pans or serving suggestions. The ingredients used in our recipes and for nutritional analyses are based on most commonly purchased foods and, unless indicated otherwise, use 2 percent reduced-fat milk, salted butter and large eggs.

A Note on Canadian Nutrition

Nutrition information is based on U.S. information. Nutrition guidelines vary in Canada. Visit Canada's Food Guide online at www.healthcanada.gc.ca/foodguide for more information.